(2)

When [...] the miracle & afterbirth [...] Let your imagination [...] the story into our own time — possibly to your own home town. A young man whose father is a carpenter grows up working in his fathers shop. He had no formal education. He owns no property of any kind. One day he walks out of his fathers shop. He starts preaching on street corners and in the country side. Walking from place to place preaching all the while even though he is in an occupied territory he never gets farther than an area perhaps 100 miles wide at the most.

He does this for 3 yrs. Then he is arrested, tried & convicted. There is no court of appeal so he is executed at age 33 along with two common thiers. Those in charge of his execution roll dice to see who gets his clothing — the only possessions he had. His family cannot afford a burial place so he is interred in a borrowed tomb.

End of story? No this uneducated, property less young man who preached on street corners for only 3 yrs. has for 2000 yrs. had a greater effect on the entire world than all the Rulers, Kings & Emperors, all the conquerors, the generals & admirals, all the scholars, scientists and philosophers who ever lived — all put together.

How do we explain that? — Unless he really was what he said he was.

This is RR Thanks for listening.

Stories in His

The Free Press
New York   London   Toronto   Sydney   Singapore

Own Hand

THE EVERYDAY WISDOM OF
RONALD REAGAN

EDITED WITH AN INTRODUCTION AND COMMENTARY BY

KIRON K. SKINNER
ANNELISE ANDERSON
MARTIN ANDERSON

Foreword by George P. Shultz

ƒP

THE FREE PRESS
A Division of Simon & Schuster, Inc.
1230 Avenue of the Americas
New York, NY 10020

Designed by Kim Llewellyn
Document photos by Brian Forrest
Manufactured in the United States of America

10   9   8   7   6   5   4   3   2   1

Library of Congress Cataloging-in-Publication Data Is Available
ISBN: 0-7432-2655-0
ISBN 9781416584506
ISBN 1-4165-8450-1

For Ronald Reagan
Who wrote the stories

Contents

Foreword

BY GEORGE P. SHULTZ

RONALD REAGAN'S talents as a storyteller are legendary. He peppered his conversations with stories. Stories lent a certain informality and ease to his speeches. He used stories to increase his rapport with the people in front of him or on the other end of the television camera. We can all remember various State of the Union Addresses where the stories involved someone sitting in the gallery with Nancy. The stories always made a point and gave drama and emphasis to the content of his speeches. He reached for stories that people could comprehend because they could imagine themselves being in the same position. He also loved jokes of all kinds. He loved the belly-laugh joke, but he was also a master of the more subtle joke that sneaks up on your funny bone from behind.

When I was serving Ronald Reagan as Secretary of State,

I would go off to Moscow with stops in various European cities or sometimes in Israel to dramatize the importance we attached to the problems of Soviet Jewry. I almost always heard new jokes on those trips. I remember once sending home what I thought was an especially illuminating cable with my analysis of some important development. I concluded the cable with a joke I had just heard. When I got home, the president remarked on the cable. Just as I thought my analysis had caught his eye, he commented on the joke. Then he told it with all sorts of embellishments and additions that made it several jokes in one. At least I knew he read my cables.

He learned from his stories and also used them to help others learn. He enjoyed the negotiating process and considered himself to be a skilled negotiator (as anyone on the Soviet side can attest). I can remember quite a few meetings with him as we discussed an upcoming negotiating session I was to have. He would frequently recall stories from his days as president of the Screen Actors Guild and as the chief negotiator with the management. He told me about an occasion when, at just the right time in those negotiations, he decided to go to the john. After a moment, who should come in but the chief management negotiator. Nobody else came in, informality reigned, and that informality provided just the right context for a candid exchange on where the negotiations might go.

Similarly, as president, Ronald Reagan always sought some way to produce an atmosphere less formal than the almost always daunting surroundings of government buildings. In 1985, his first meeting with Mikhail Gorbachev started, as he had arranged, with the two of them sitting in front of a fireplace in the main house we were using. Later, at a break in the afternoon discussion, he suggested that the two of them leave for a while and walk down to the lake where there was a small house with a roaring fire in the fireplace. He came back triumphantly announcing that they had agreed on home and home visits. Somehow, the informality had worked. So had the timing.

Along with his great sense of timing, Ronald Reagan used stories and jokes effectively to make points, to loosen up the atmosphere, and to create a sense of informality. But I don't believe I ever heard him tell what people would classify as a "dirty joke."

One joke he told to Mikhail Gorbachev—but not until toward the end of the Moscow summit in 1988 when their relationship was a pretty good one—illustrates his style. One of Gorbachev's first actions as the new Secretary General in Moscow was to crack down on the sale of vodka. He felt, certainly with good reason, that the people of the Soviet Union drank too much, so he made it difficult to get vodka. A short while after his program started, according to a story circulating in Moscow, two guys were standing in line at the vodka store. They were there for a half hour, then an hour, then an hour and a half. Finally, one said to the other, "I'm sick of this. I'm going over to the Kremlin to shoot Gorbachev." He left. About an hour later, he returned and found his buddy still in line. His friend asked, "Well, did you shoot him?" He replied, "Hell, no. The line up there is a lot longer than this one." Gorbachev's uneasy smile in response to Reagan's joke perhaps betrayed some increased appreciation of the limits of regimentation.

Freedom, patriotism, faith, and optimism all are on display in these stories, which run the gamut from sports to philosophy, from illness to courage, always with deep respect for the ingenuity and capacity of the human being.

Yes, Ronald Reagan was a great communicator, a skillful user of stories with a real point. But the deeper point is the depth and content he was forever putting before us.

Take your time with this book. It's short and easy—also profound.

Introduction

DURING OUR RESEARCH in Ronald Reagan's private papers at the Ronald Reagan Presidential Library, we found an extraordinary number of handwritten documents that have proven highly revealing about the man and his political career. Most of those manuscripts focus on policy issues and demonstrate that Reagan read widely and worked hard to determine clear positions on virtually every major policy issue, both domestic and foreign. Some of his other writings are very different in nature. Whether personal stories, anecdotes he first heard elsewhere, or even jokes, they are less about public policy than virtue and values, love and loss, courage, ingenuity, tenacity, and religious faith.

In this book, we present thirty stories Reagan wrote for his daily national radio program in the late 1970s and six sto-

One enduring myth is that Reagan napped on the plane during his political campaigns. Never was true. As soon as the plane took off, he was working—reading and writing. Accompanied by one of his advisers, Martin Anderson, he is at work in 1975 on a Lear jet during the pre-presidential campaign.

ries he wrote at other points in his life. The stories reveal more about Reagan's character than his policies, and they are crucial to understanding his life and career.

Most of the stories in this book are true accounts of people's lives. We found newspaper or magazine articles or other corroborating material for all of the stories we checked. For instance, the first story in this book, "Life and Death," is based on the short life of a boy in Santa Barbara. *The Santa Barbara News Press* carried an article about the boy. We found also all of the books that Reagan refers to in his stories.

During Reagan's presidency, many of his aides heard him tell jokes and talk about his early years. We present President Reagan's *handwritten* versions of those stories.

Some of the stories in the files of Reagan's handwritten drafts are based on folklore. We chose a few of them for this book.

Reagan rarely told a story that did not have a point, though not everyone appreciated it. Whenever he said, "Well, that reminds me of . . . ," it was wise to listen closely to understand how he felt about something, and listeners who assumed he was changing or avoiding a subject did so at their peril. The stories published here reveal his faith in people of all walks of life, even—perhaps particularly—when they were oppressed by circumstance. The stories also reveal Reagan's natural affection for his fellow man, his enthusiasm for adventure and fun, and his compassion. He tells jokes at his own expense, poking fun at his misdeeds as a youth. He speaks repeatedly of the importance of faith in his own life and the lives of others.

To many people, Reagan was an enigma. He did not seem to work hard. He seemed never to question himself or his policies. Yet his presidency was one of the most significant in the twentieth century. And his standing with the American people continues to rise. The man and his political career cannot be explained entirely by his political philosophy or his specific policies. These stories fill a crucial gap.

Reagan was most comfortable and relaxed when working his ranch, dressed in Levi's, boots, and a cowboy hat. One of his strengths was that, no matter how far he rose in politics, he could happily trade it all for his ranch in Santa Barbara County, high in the mountains overlooking the Pacific Ocean.

Note on Methods

IN OUR EARLIER BOOK, *Reagan, In His Own Hand,* we reproduced the full rough drafts that Reagan wrote, showing all of his insertions, deletions, and other editing. In this book, to make the reading smoother, we simply present the final handwritten draft that Reagan produced without showing any of his editing. We also use conventional spelling and capitalization and expand his abbreviations.

However, we reproduce full facsimiles of seven of the stories in the book and they show the exact editing of the rough drafts of Reagan's writings. Moreover, we are preparing a second volume of *Reagan, In His Own Hand* which will contain approximately 450 more essays, all displaying Reagan's editing—and the stories in this book will be included in that volume with full editing shown.

Life and Death

REAGAN'S RADIO COMMENTARIES ABOUT A YOUNG BOY AND A FATHER'S LETTER TO HIS SON AT WAR ARE STORIES ABOUT DEATH AS AN EXTENSION OF LIFE.

Life and Death
February 20, 1978

No matter how many times we say that death is a normal part of living, a part of God's plan for all of us, we still tend to be shocked and grieved when it comes to those near and dear to us. Now let me hasten to make plain that of course we feel grief and sorrow when a loved one leaves us. But that sorrow is for ourselves because of the loss in our own lives of a beloved companion.

But I'm speaking of the grief, the regret, we feel for the

Every now & then something occurs to remind us
that how you live is of far greater importance than
how long you live. I'll be right back.

No matter how many times we say that death is a
normal part of living, a part of God's plan for all
of us, we still tend to be shocked and grieved when
it comes to those near & dear to us. Now let me
hasten to make plain that of course we feel grief
and sorrow when a loved one leaves us. ~~There~~ But
~~that~~ sorrow ~~is for us~~ because of the loss in our own
lives of a beloved companion.

But I'm speaking of the grief ~~and regret~~ we feel for the person
who has had to depart this life. We speak of the waste
of the deceased is young and has not lived out his allotted
more than 3 score & 10. And all to ~~say~~ ~~of us~~ said,
~~to~~ to wonder that if our Judeo-Christian tradition
means anything, ~~that~~ the departure has simply moved
on to what we've been ~~told~~ promised is a better life.

A few weeks ago a little boy died in Santa
Barbara Calif. His life span a mere 7 years before
Leukemia took him. We have to feel sorrow for the
Mother & Father ~~whose dreams~~ for him ended so
quickly but surely his lonely trial has served a
purpose every bit as much as if his life had been
measured in decades not years.

At 7 years he is described as having an unusual
understanding of suffering & of God. A volunteer with a group which works with
the dying & their families recorded (at Edwards's request)
his thoughts about dying & even his wishes as to his
funeral. In answer to a question as to why he
wanted to die (you see he had asked the doctor to
disconnect the life support systems) he said, "Because
I am so sick. When you are dead & a spirit
in heaven you don't have all the aches & pains.

And sometimes if you want to, you can visit that
life - but you cant come back into your own life. If you
dont hang on to your body & let yourself save away, it is not
so painful. "Death is like a passage way, a road into another galaxy."
These are the words - the wise words of
a 7 yr. old boy. He went on to say "Sometimes Dr's
want to save people very badly. They try everything to
cure them." I dont feel good and I am too sick to live
on".

His mother tells the final moment. He said "Mother
turn off the oxygen, I dont need it anymore." She did as
he asked and says "I turned it off then he held my
hand and a big smile came to his face and he said 'It
is time'." "Then he left".

His mother summed it all up when she said "It was
a privilege & an honor to go through this with my son.
I hope it helps parents talk things over with their
children & doctors. If he's done this in his short life,
then it will have been worth it".

We can all learn from a very remarkable 7 yr. old boy
and surely his life had meaning for all of us.
       This is R.R. Thanks for listening.

person who has had to depart this life. We speak of the waste if the deceased is young and has not lived out his or her more than three-score-and-ten. And all too often we fail to remember that if our Judeo-Christian tradition means anything, the departed has simply moved on to what we've been assured is a better life.

A few weeks ago a little boy died in Santa Barbara, California. His life span a mere seven years before leukemia took him. We have to feel sorrow for the mother and father whose dreams for him ended so quickly but surely his brief time here served a purpose every bit as much as if his life had been measured in decades not years.

At seven years he is described as having an unusual understanding of suffering and of God. A volunteer with a group which works with the dying and their families recorded (at Edouardo's request) his thoughts about dying and even his wishes as to his funeral. In answer to a question as to why he wanted to die—(you see he had asked the doctors to disconnect the life support systems) he said, "Because I am so sick. When you are dead and a spirit in heaven you don't have all the aches and pains. And sometimes if you want to, you can visit this life but you can't come back into your own life. If you don't hang on to your body and let yourself ease away it is not so painful. Death is like a passageway, a walk into another galaxy." These are the words—the wise words of a seven-year-old boy. He went on to say, "Sometimes doctors want to save people very badly. They try everything to cure them. I don't feel good and I am too sick to live on."

His mother tells of the final moment. He said, "Mother turn off the oxygen. I don't need it anymore." She did as he asked and says, "I turned it off then he held my hand and a big smile came to his face and he said 'It is time.' Then he left."

His mother summed it all up when she said, "It was a privilege and an honor to go through this with my son. I hope it helps parents talk things over with their children and doctors. If he's done this in his short life, then it will have been worth it."

We can all learn from a very remarkable seven-year-old boy and surely his life had meaning for all of us.

Father and Son
January 27, 1978

Not too long ago on one of these broadcasts I quoted an anonymous source to the effect that if all of us knew on a certain day the world was ending, the roads, streets and telephone lines would be jammed with people trying to reach someone to say "I love you." Since then some of you have written to express agreement with that unknown author. And some have begun a sentence with the words, "If only I had"—or "hadn't" as the case might be.

Back in World War II a father wrote a letter to his soldier son in the form of a poem:

In the late 1970s, when Reagan wrote radio commentaries, he used to save the manuscripts until he had written fifteen. After they were typed, he would record them in a studio. A record, each containing fifteen of his commentaries, was then sent to over three hundred radio stations, where one selection was played every weekday for three weeks—reaching millions of listeners.

Dear Son:

I wish I had the power to write
The thoughts wedged in my heart tonight
As I sit watching that small star
And wondering where and how you are.
You know, Son, it's a funny thing
How close a war can really bring
A Father, who for years with pride,
Has kept emotions deep inside.
I'm sorry, Son, when you were small
I let reserve build up that wall;
I told you real men never cried,
And it was Mom who always dried
Your tears and smoothed your hurts away
So that you soon went back to play.
But, Son, deep down within my heart
I longed to have some little part
In drying that small tear-stained face,
But we were men—men don't embrace.
And suddenly I found my Son
A full grown man, with childhood done.
Tonight you're far across the sea,
Fighting a war for men like me.

Well, somehow pride and what is right
Have each changed places here tonight.
I find my eyes won't stay quite dry
And that men sometimes really cry.
And if we stood here, face to face
I'm sure, my Son, we would embrace.
Son, Dads are quite a funny lot,
And if I've failed you on some spot
It's not because I loved you less
But just this cussed manliness.
And if I had the power to write
The thoughts wedged in my heart tonight,
The words would ring out loud and true,
I'm proud, my Son, yes proud of you.

He signed it "Dad" and walked down to the corner and dropped it in the mailbox. As he returned home and reached his own doorstep he was handed the war department telegram, the one that began with the fateful words "We regret to inform you."

I'm glad that I can believe his son knew he had written that letter.

Love and Compassion

IN THESE STORIES LOVE AND COMPASSION HELP PEO-
PLE COPE WITH DIRE PERSONAL CIRCUMSTANCES AND
OVERCOME SEEMINGLY IMPOSSIBLE ODDS.

*Reagan invokes the observations of Alexis de Tocqueville and
tells a story to make the point that the voluntary associations
that people form to solve their problems are part of the uniqueness and strength of America.*

Charity
March 23, 1977

Some 130 or 140 years ago a French philosopher came to
America to see at first hand what he called "this great experi-

ment." He's probably been quoted in these modern days more by after dinner speakers than any other individual.

Going back to France he wrote a book about democracy in America. He said he had sought for the greatness of America in her commodious harbors and her ample rivers and it was not there. Nor did he find it in our rich mines and vast world commerce. He wrote, "Not until I went to the churches of America and heard her pulpits aflame with righteousness did I understand the secret of her genius and her power. America is great because she is good and if America ever ceases to be good, America will cease to be great."

In his book he told his countrymen how in America a citizen would see a problem that needed solving; that he wouldn't call on the government but would cross the street and talk to a neighbor. They would talk to others and soon a committee would be formed, the problem would be solved and as de Tocqueville said, "You won't believe this but no government bureau will be involved at all."

Our French visitor of more than a century ago would have been reassured if he had been in Santa Barbara, California a short time ago. A young girl barely in her teens faced certain death from a form of leukemia. Her chance for life depended on the relatively new and unusual procedure of bone marrow transplant. The operation and accompanying treatment available in a medical center in Minnesota costs tens of thousands of dollars. Money which her family didn't have.

Word got around. Then the local media broke the story.

Someone proposed forming a committee. I can't recount all the efforts that were put forth but Fess Parker organized a symphony concert, the proceeds of which went into the fund. McDonald's contributed the food for a benefit dinner. School children mobilized and went door to door soliciting contributions and as de Tocqueville more than a century ago said, "before you knew it the problem was solved"—solved by a spontaneous community effort.

The tens of thousands of dollars were raised and the young lady thanks to neighbors and friends she didn't know she had is in Minnesota. There is more. It seems that more than enough money was raised than will be needed. So— those who engaged in this good work have decided to use the surplus as the beginning of a permanent fund for future needs of this kind.

I know this isn't the first such incident and I know that whenever and wherever people have learned of such a problem they have responded in a like manner.

The youngsters who spent their after school hours on the door to door solicitation have had an experience they will take with them into adulthood. They will always remember the good feeling that was theirs so that when time comes for them to take over they too will, "cross over the street and talk to a neighbor," about the problem that needs solving. "The quality of mercy is not strained it falleth as the gentle rain from Heaven,"—a good thing for everyone to know and remember.

A young woman's love and compassion defy human odds.

Wedding
July 1978

On Sunday July 15th in Chicago Linda Fraschalla walked down the aisle and was married to Pete Saraceno. As they led the wedding party from the church the pace was a little slow because Pete had to use a walker.

Actually the marriage itself was about two years late. Linda and Pete had planned to wed in 1976 right after he was released from the Marines. Then Pete and a buddy crashed an automobile. Pete was critically injured and pronounced dead on arrival at Westlake Hospital. But a doctor felt for a pulse one last time and found a very faint one. Pete was alive, but in a coma.

After twelve days in a respirator and with five other life support machines attached to him the doctors told his mother to pull the plug. She replied that if God had wanted him, he would have taken him in the accident. He would remain in the coma for 3½ months. At three months he contracted double pneumonia and was given only a few hours to live.

Linda works in the admitting office at Presbyterian–St. Luke's Hospital. Every night after work she visited Pete who never so much as moved an eyelash. Nevertheless Linda was there decorating his room with a lighted tree for Christmas, spending New Year's Eve with him. Sympathetic doctors told her to go out, have fun and try to forget him. She refused.

Reagan at the height of his power, dressed in black tie, smiling confidently, toasting with a crystal glass of champagne.

Then one day Pete opened his eyes and his eyes began following Linda as she moved around the room. Later a finger moved, then an arm and finally he tried to speak. Linda was the only one who could understand him. Even when he made no sound she could read his lips.

He spent seven months at Westlake, then to the Chicago Rehabilitation Institute and finally home. Linda quit her job and used her savings to buy a 28-foot backyard swimming pool to help him exercise his legs.

One day his mother took him back to Westlake to meet the nurses who had cared for him during the long months of coma. He stepped off the third floor elevator using a walker and Mrs. Saraceno says there wasn't a dry eye on the floor.

When Pete asked Linda's father for permission to marry her Mr. Fraschalla said, "When you can walk down that aisle, she's all yours."

Linda has returned to her job but has spent her evenings decorating a garden type apartment in Melrose Park where they are now at home. Pete had wanted to become a Chicago policeman but still has trouble with his left arm. Linda says he can do some kind of desk work.

Pete says, "The doctors call me the miracle boy and I guess they are right. I'm lucky to be alive and I'm lucky to have Linda." Yes he is. When the doctors told Linda that he would never make it, she told them "I love him," and she refused to believe them. She said, "I wanted to help him so I stayed at his side as much as I could." Pete says, "She sure taught me about love." I think she taught all of us something Pete. Congratulations. And to you Linda a lifetime of love and happiness.

Faith and Religion

"NOW FAITH IS THE SUBSTANCE OF THINGS HOPED FOR, THE EVIDENCE OF THINGS NOT SEEN. . . . THROUGH FAITH WE UNDERSTAND THAT THE WORLDS WERE FRAMED BY THE WORD OF GOD, SO THAT THINGS WHICH ARE SEEN WERE NOT MADE OF THINGS WHICH DO APPEAR." (HEBREWS 11:1–3). THROUGH RELIGIOUS STORIES, REAGAN REVEALS HIS VIEWS ABOUT FAITH, THE LIFE OF JESUS CHRIST, AND THE JUDEO-CHRISTIAN TRADITION.

Christmas
January 9, 1978

All the traditions associated with Christmas were observed as usual in the past holiday season including the chorus of complaints that over-commercialization is robbing the day of its true meaning. I'll have to confess I can't join that chorus. Somehow the ads offering helpful gift suggestions when we are all filled with the spirit of giving, the decorations on the streets and in the stores, the familiar carols add to the Christmas spirit for me and don't really strike me as crass or insensitive money grubbing.

I am disturbed however about something I read over the holidays which could *really* rob Christmas of its meaning for millions of us who see it as more than just the birthday of a great and good teacher. I realize there are those who by religious belief consider Jesus a very human prophet whose teachings about love for one another, treating others as we would like to be treated ourselves are sound patterns for living; that he is to be respected but not worshiped.

But for many of us he is much more. He is the promised Messiah, the Son of God come to earth to offer salvation for all mankind. It was disturbing therefore to read that in many Christian seminaries there is an increasing tendency to minimize his divinity, to reject the miracle of his birth and regard him as merely human.

Meaning no disrespect to the religious convictions of others I still can't help wondering how we can explain away what to me is the greatest miracle of all and which is recorded in history. No one denies there was such a man, that he lived and that he was put to death by crucifixion.

Where then you may ask is the miracle I spoke of? Well consider this and let your imagination if you will translate the story into our own time—possibly to your own home town.

A young man whose father is a carpenter grows up working in his father's shop. He has no formal education. He owns no property of any kind. One day he puts down his tools and walks out of his father's shop. He starts preaching on street corners and in the nearby countryside. Walking from place to place preaching all the while even though he is in no way an ordained minister he never gets farther than an area perhaps 100 miles wide at the most.

He does this for three years. Then he is arrested, tried and convicted. There is no court of appeal so he is executed at age 33 along with two common thieves. Those in charge of his execution roll dice to see who gets his clothing—the only possessions he has. His family cannot afford a burial place so he is interred in a borrowed tomb.

End of story? No this uneducated, propertyless young man who preached on street corners for only three years who left no written word has for 2000 years had a greater effect on the entire world than all the rulers, kings and emperors, all the conquerors, the generals and admirals, all the scholars, scientists and philosophers who ever lived—all put together.

How do we explain that?—Unless he really was what he said he was.

Mirages
July 15, 1978

I suppose it's only natural for any of us regardless of our faith to speculate at times as to whether or not there might be a natural explanation for some of the biblical miracles. I'll confess to doing it in idle thought on occasion but always winding up unable to explain away the happening described in either the Old or New Testaments as natural phenomena.

But today just as there are revisionists trying to rewrite history so are there scholars—yes and theologians trying to de-spiritualize the Judeo-Christian tradition. Some time ago I commented on this with regard to the Christmas story.

Now a scholar has come up with a scientific explanation of two of the better known miracles. He says they were simply mirages. The first is the parting of the Red Sea which allowed Moses and the Israelites to escape the pursuing Egyptians and the second is Jesus walking on the waters of the Sea of Galilee.

Most of us know something about mirages, particularly those of us who live in the West. And I dare say most of us have been driving on a hot day and seen the highway ahead take on the appearance of water shining in the sunlight. We don't put on the brakes because we know it is simply heat waves rising from the pavement giving the illusion of water. Of course there is much more scientific knowledge about the often-elaborate mirages and reflected images seen in desert areas and I'll admit I'm not blessed with that knowledge.

But this scholar who is has suggested that the Israelites were simply led across desert sands at a time when a mirage gave them the appearance of walking through water.

As I say I'm not an informed scholar on the subject of mirages. But even giving the writer that edge I'm still left with

Mirages

Some one has come up with a scientific explanation for some of the miracles recorded in both the old & new Testaments. I'll be right back.

I suppose it's only natural for any of us regardless of our faith to speculate at times ~~as to whether or not~~ ~~miracles recorded in the Bible could~~ there might be a natural explanation for some of the biblical miracles. I'll confess to doing it in idle thought on occasion but always winding up unable to explain away the happening ~~as it~~ described in either the old or new Testament as natural phenomena.

But today just as there are revisionists trying to re-write history so are there scholars — yes theologians trying to de-spiritualize the Judeo-Christian tradition. Some time ago I commented on this with regard to the Christmas story.

Now a scholar has come up with a scientific explanation of two of the better known miracles. He says they were simply mirages. The first is the parting of the Red Sea which allowed ~~the~~ Moses & the Israelites to escape the pursuing Egyptians and the second is Jesus walking on the waters of the sea of ~~Galilee~~ Galilee.

Most of us know something about mirages, particularly those of us who live in the West. And I dare say most of us have been driving on a hot day & seen the highway ahead take on the appearance of water shining in the sun light. We don't put on the brakes because we know it is simply heat waves rising from the pavement ~~and~~ giving the illusion of water. Of course there is much more scientific knowledge about the often elaborate mirages & reflected images ~~that~~ in desert areas and I dare say I'm not blessed with that knowledge.

But this scholar who is has suggested that the

Israelites were simply and across desert sands at a time when a mirage gave them the appearance of walking through water. ~~K~~ ~~~~~~

And say I'm not an informed scholar on the subject of mirages. ~~~~~~~~~~~~~~~~~~~~~~~~~~~~~~~~~ But even giving the writer that much I'm still left with some questions. The mirage might (and let me emphasize THE WORD "might") explain the Israelites crossing ~~at~~ the Red Sea but that leaves the story very much complicated. The Armies of the Pharaoh tried to pursue & the waters closed on them crushing chariots & drowning men & horses. ~~~~~~~~~~~~~~~~~~~~~~~~~~~~~~~~ A mirage can do that? ~~~~~~~~~~~~~~~~~~

There's (that) an unanswered question or two about Jesus walking on water if we assume he was on dry land & part of a mirage. First of all it was night and the Disciples were in a wave tossed boat. Jesus walked from the shore to join ~~them in the boat~~. If that was a mirage & he was really on dry land — what was that boat doing there?

I'm afraid our scholar has asked too much of heat waves & reflections on cloud & desert sand. It will take more than a mirage to do a successful re-write of the all time world's best seller — the Bible.

Thank you R.R. Thanks for history.

some questions. The mirage might (and let me emphasize the word might) explain the Israelites crossing the Red Sea but that leaves the story very much unfinished. The armies of the Pharaoh tried to follow and the waters closed on them crushing chariots and drowning men and horses. A mirage can do that?

Then there is an unanswered question or two about Jesus walking on the water if we assume he was on dry land and part of a mirage. First of all it was night and the Disciples were in a wave tossed boat. Jesus walked from the shore to join them in the boat. If that was a mirage and he was really on dry land—what was the boat doing there?

I'm afraid our scholar has asked too much of heat waves and reflections on cloud and desert sand. It will take more than a mirage to do a successful rewrite of the all-time world's best seller—the Bible.

In a letter written during the middle of his presidency, Reagan declares his belief in the power of intercessory prayer.

Letter to Sister Mary Ignatius
November 26, 1984

To Sister Mary Ignatius DMJ
Dear Sister Mary Ignatius

Nancy and I are deeply grateful for your warm letter and card congratulating us on having our option taken up. We are as always even more grateful for your prayers in our be-

half. I believe in intercessory prayer and know I have bene-
fited from it. I have, of course, added my own prayers to the
point that sometimes I wonder if the Lord doesn't say, "here
he comes again."

Abe Lincoln once said that he would be the most stupid
human on this footstool called earth if he thought for one
minute he could fulfill the obligations of the office he held
without help from one who was wiser and stronger than all
others. I understand what he meant completely—and if
that is mixing politics and religion then it is a good and
proper mix.

Again you have our heartfelt thanks.

Sincerely
RR

Sports and Religion
March 2, 1977

A few weeks ago having covered the news section, then the
comics and the editorial page of the morning paper (and I do
it in that order) I turned to the sports section. This doesn't
mean that sports come last on my list of priorities—far from
it. I'm just a creature of habit, set in my ways.

My eye was caught by a four column photo of a basketball team and coach on the bench, heads bowed or resting on
their crossed arms. I read the caption thinking this must be a
team that had just suffered a terrible defeat. I was wrong.
Their heads were bowed not in grief but in prayer. They play

under the title "Athletes In Action"—(AIA) and as the caption writer couldn't resist pointing out they are a team that prays together and plays together.

AIA, the sports arm of Campus Crusade for Christ, is headquartered in Tustin, California and hopes to represent the United States at the world championships in Manila in 1978. They may very well make it. Recently they overwhelmed the country's top ranked team, University of San Francisco, 104 to 85, then rode over Nevada Las Vegas (also high ranked) 104 to 77. Nevada went into the game averaging 53 rebounds a game—they got only 33 and AIA had 64.

This is an amateur team and plays colleges and universities who can take the defeats handed them because they don't appear in their win, lose record. AIA's record at the time of the photo was 78 wins 14 losses. Total record—they are 25–6 for the season—all on the road. They have no home base.

One of their players turned down a no cut two-year contract with a pro team that would have brought him $230,000. There are other former university stars who were high draft choices for pro ball. Their income is $700 if single, $900 if married and it is not for playing basketball.

They are ministers. When half-time comes they don't go to the locker room for the coach's input on what to do in the second half. They towel themselves off, pick up microphones and tell the crowd of their belief in God.

The news article said the reaction is mixed. Sometimes they get attentive audiences but sometimes on college campuses they are booed, jeered and cursed by small but noisy groups. As one of them said though, "We just try to rise above it." And they must succeed because between two and three thousand people have responded to their half-time messages by accepting God. In addition another 10,000 have responded by mail asking for more information.

Wherever they are, at home or on the road they address civic groups or speak in churches and hold clinics in high schools and with coaches. And all the time they have a basketball team that some say could go up against the pros and give a good account of itself. After all they have beaten the number one college team and in the Midwest broke a 48-game home winning streak of another top ranked university team.

They have a faith that has enabled them to gamble that they can buy TV time for thousands of dollars and put their games on television as delayed telecasts. I'm going to start looking for them; they just may be the best amateur team in the country and can get even better. Some of the nation's top stars are interested in joining them when their college days are over and the bait isn't basketball it's faith in God.

What has Karl Marx wrought? Reagan says Marx spawned a political method that completely destroys religious freedom.

Religious Freedom
July 31, 1978

I think sometimes there is a built in optimism in Americans that makes us want to believe that things are all right in other lands and other places. Perhaps it is this happy outlook that makes us accept the stories of returning travelers from behind the iron or the bamboo curtains.

There is plenty of evidence indicating that visitors to the various "workers' paradises" are treated to showcase tours but carefully kept from seeing things as they really are. Of late we've had the make believe exposed by visitors to Cuba, China and elsewhere who, with courage and persistence risked possible imprisonment to look behind the false front.

One of the more prevalent myths has to do with religious freedom and whether it does or does not exist in those lands where Karl Marx is hailed as the Messiah. The World Council of Churches seems unable to believe that religion might be forbidden fruit in the communist world. The fact that a few churches in Russia remain open and are attended by an ever shrinking group of senior citizens makes the Council ignore the uncompromising Marxian denial of God.

He swore that his paradise could only be realized by destroying the church. He had a special hatred for the Hebrews, possibly because the God of Moses is also the God of Christianity.

Not too long ago Austrian journalists got hold of an examination being given school children in Czechoslovakia. They made their findings public and it does seem to answer those who have denied that communism and religious persecution go hand in hand.

There are fifteen questions in the examination but I think three are enough to settle any argument. In giving the test the students are instructed that they are to answer "correctly, truthfully and honestly." Question one: "If you are religious, are you aware that your religious rating will form a serious obstruction with a view to your future career?" If that isn't discouraging enough try this one: "Our school is educating you as a skilled worker of the future. Since you will participate in the leadership of the production process, your attitude toward religion must be clear. For this reason the school has the right to influence your religious attitude and your feelings in respect to your future job. Does the school—the teaching staff—do this with conviction? Answer yes or no."

Now if that one isn't enough to put little Ivan's teacher on notice here is sample number three. "During your term of study at the school, was enough insight and help given in the battle against religion and its pressures, and in the formation of a scientific view of the world?"

So much for religious freedom in the world of communism. I doubt that many children behind the curtains treasure gold stars for Sunday school attendance.

Women and Men

WOMEN WERE DRAWN TO REAGAN, AND PERHAPS
FOR REASONS THAT WENT BEYOND HIS GOOD LOOKS.
A SURPRISING ASPECT OF HIS CHARACTER IS HIS
DEEP RESPECT FOR THE STRENGTH AND TOUGHNESS
OF WOMEN. HE NEVER THOUGHT WOMEN WERE LIKE
MEN. IN SOME WAYS REAGAN FEELS WOMEN ARE SU-
PERIOR, CALLING THEM "THE SINGLE MOST CIVILIZ-
ING INFLUENCE IN THE WORLD."

Women
May 15, 1978

In spite of all the jokes men like to tell about women drivers
I think almost all men know in their hearts that women have
been the single most civilizing influence in the world.

Years ago I read of an incident that took place in India during the days of British colonial rule. It is not a make believe legend but an actual happening. I was reminded of it on our recent trip and thought you might like to hear it.

The scene is a dinner party in one of the palatial homes in India, a typical cosmopolitan gathering including a British colonel of the old school and a visiting American businessman. The rest were colonials, Indian notables and so forth.

Somehow the conversation had gotten around to heroics, courage and what makes individuals perform noble deeds. The British colonel was holding forth on the idea that men have that extra bit of control which in time of stress makes them able to resist panic and with courage do the dangerous thing that has to be done. Women on the other hand, according to the Colonel are not gifted with that measure of control and therefore grow hysterical, faint or stand helpless to act in the face of danger.

As he was going on in that vein the American happened to notice the hostess signal to one of the servants who leaned over her chair while she whispered something to him. The American thought nothing of this until he saw the servant returning to the room carrying a saucer of milk. Passing the table he set the saucer on the floor just outside the glass doors which opened onto the patio. Suddenly the American remembered,—in India a saucer of milk is snake bait—cobra bait to be exact.

He saw the servants standing against the dining room

In all this time of womens lib and controversy
over womens place in the world I happen to believe if it
weren't for the ladies we men would still be carrying clubs.

I'll be right back.

In spite of all the jokes men like to tell about
women drivers I think almost all men know in
their hearts that women have been the single most
civilizing influence in the world.

Years ago I read of an incident that took
place in India during the days of British Colonial
rule. It is not a make believe legend but an actual
happening. I was reminded of it on our recent trip
and thought you might like to hear it.

The scene is a dinner party in one of the
palatial homes in India, a typical cosmopolitan
gathering including a British Col of the old school and
a visiting American business man. The rest were Colonials,
Indian notables etc.

Somehow the conversation had gotten around to
heroics, courage and what makes individuals perform
noble deeds. The British Col. was holding forth on the
idea that men have that extra bit of control which
in time of stress makes them able to resist panic
and with courage do the dangerous thing that has to
be done. Women on the other hand, according to the
Col. are not gifted with that measure of control and
therefore grow hysterical, faint or stand helpless to act
in the face of danger.

As he was going on in that vein the American
happened to noted the hostess signaled one of the servants who
leaned over her chair while she whispered something to
him. The American thought nothing of this until he
saw the servant returning to the room carrying a
saucer of milk. Passing the table he set the saucer
on the floor just outside the glass doors which opened

on to the patio. Suddenly ^(The American) remembered, ^(in India) a saucer of milk is snake bait - Cobra bait to be exact.

He saw the servants standing against the dining room wall and it was obvious they were frightened & tense. Quickly he looked around the room. There was no furniture that could conceal a snake. He looked over head thinking possibly it could be on a beam but there were no beams, it was a tile vaulted ceiling.

Then he realized there was only one possible place a snake could be — under the table. His first instinct was to push his chair back and run but he knew this could cause the snake to strike one of the other guests. The Col. was still holding forth. The American interrupted him & said, "Col. let's have a test and see who has the most control. Let's see how many of us can remain absolutely silent & motionless for 5 min. I'll count to 300 as a measure of the time and no one must move or utter a sound.

Everyone went along with the idea and the count down started. It had reached 280 when a King Cobra slithered from beneath the table and through the patio doors to the saucer of milk. The servants slammed the doors with the snake on the outside.

In the excitement that followed the Col. shouted, "That proves my point, this man could have saved himself but he thought of a plan to save the rest of us". The American said, "Just a minute Col." turning to the hostess he asked "How did you know there was a Cobra under the table?" She said, "It was on my foot".

This is RR Thanks for listening.

wall and it was obvious they were frightened and tense. Quickly he looked around the room. There was no furniture that could conceal a snake. He looked overhead thinking possibly it could be on a beam but there were no beams, it was a tile vaulted ceiling.

Then he realized there was only one possible place a snake could be—under the table. His first instinct was to push his chair back and run but he knew this could cause the snake to strike one of the other guests. The Colonel was still holding forth. The American interrupted him and said, "Colonel let's have a test and see who has the most control. Let's see how many of us can remain absolutely silent and motionless for five minutes. I'll count to 300 as a measure of the time and no one must move or utter a sound."

Everyone went along with the idea and the countdown started. It had reached 280 when a king cobra slithered from beneath the table and through the patio doors to the saucer of milk. The servants slammed the doors with the snake on the outside.

In the excitement that followed the Colonel shouted, "That proves my point, this man could have saved himself but he thought of a plan to save the rest of us." The American said, "Just a minute Colonel." Turning to the hostess he asked, "How did you know there was a cobra under the table?" She said, "It was on my foot."

Women's March
September 1, 1976

There is a savagery loose in the world. . . .

One of the most tragic trouble spots is Northern Ireland where for seven years neighbor has taken the life of neighbor and done so in the name of God—the same God prayed to by both sides. There is a non-sectarian issue to be sure; the argument as to whether Northern Ireland should remain under British rule or become part of the Irish Republic. But the religious difference is very real and lends an extra special bitterness to the dispute.

Just when you would think the killing had become so commonplace as to be endured something happened a few weeks ago that resulted in a kind of miracle. During these seven years bombs have been exploded in crowded taverns and department stores, cold blooded executions have taken place and continual sniping has added to the toll. Then a few weeks ago three children of one family were killed by the I.R.A. Ironically killer or killers and victims were on the same side. The children weren't the targets as far as is known. They just happened to be in the way when the guns talked.

One woman—aunt to the three children—spoke to another woman. Then the two set out to speak to others. Only days after the funeral a meeting of two or three thousand women took place. They demanded an end to the killing and called on women everywhere to join them.

It has always been my belief that women brought civilization to the world. Without their influence we males would still be carrying clubs and in recent years we've come pretty close to doing that again.

Just days ago 30,000 women from both sides Catholic and Protestant marched through Belfast voicing one demand, "stop killing our children." In Dublin 20,000 marched in sympathy, smaller groups did so in other Irish towns. In Belfast stones were hurled at them—by men of course, young men. They kept on marching. Women stepped off the sidewalks to join them. They ask their sisters all over the world to join them, to rally for an end to the killing.

What if it happens? Imagine the men in the Kremlin if they looked down on Russia's women marching in the streets demanding peace. Why not? Does anyone have a better idea?

Race Relations

REAGAN'S FIRST "REAL JOLT" WITH RACIAL BIGOTRY OCCURRED IN THE EARLY 1930S WHILE HE WAS IN COLLEGE. IN A 1981 INTERVIEW WITH JOURNALIST MARK SHIELDS, HE TELLS US WHAT HE DID ABOUT IT. THE OTHER TWO STORIES IN THIS SECTION ARE EULOGIES FOR BLACK AMERICANS WHOM REAGAN KNEW.

Reagan and Race in the 1930s

From *Inside Sports*
March 31, 1981

IS: Mr. President, I had lunch with Franklin Burghardt, who played with you in college, and he told an interesting story. The Eureka College team was on the road and scheduled to check into a hotel that turned out to be for whites only. They weren't going to let the black players stay with the rest of the team in the hotel. And a fellow named Reagan talked to the coach about making other arrangements. Do you remember that?

REAGAN: I remember it, but I didn't know that we hadn't fooled Burgie. I knew everybody in town, which was about 15 miles from where we were to play, so I went in with the coach to introduce him to the hotel manager. And the hotel manager said he would take everyone but Burghardt and the other black on the team. So our coach said, "Well then, we're going someplace else." And the manager said, "I think I might as well tell you that no other hotel will either."

Now, I was horrified. I suppose it was one of the first real jolts I'd had about this thing. It's what I meant when I said that I grew up in an era when the country didn't even know it had a racial problem. This wasn't the Deep South—this was northern Illinois. And this was being said to our teammates. Our coach was so mad that he said, "We'll sleep in the bus." And I stopped him then, which wasn't easy because I had that feeling that a fellow frequently has for a coach—you don't argue with him. But I said, "Mac, if you do that it will be worse for them [the blacks]. They'll feel that everyone has been made uncomfortable because of them. Why don't you go out and tell them that you can only take part of the squad in here." He had previously told me that I would have to stay with the squad, that I couldn't go home—there in my hometown. So I said, "Tell them that we're going to have to split up. Then I'll take the two of them home." And, mad as he was about it, he looked at me kind of wide-eyed and said, "You, really . . . ?" And I said, "Well, yes, of course. No problem."

IS: That was not a common occurrence in those days.

REAGAN: No. But I knew my folks. I'd been raised with a hatred for bigotry. Because my father was Catholic and my mother was Protestant, I knew what it was like to go to school and hear the kids talking about the Catholic church; the basement being full of guns for the day when the Pope was going to conquer America. And, God bless them, my parents never even blinked. I got there with my two black teammates and I told my mother there wasn't enough room in the hotel for all of us.

IS: Dr. Burghardt remembers it well.

REAGAN: I didn't know Burgie ever knew that. . . . You know in those days, if you had a black playing on your team and the other team didn't, he took an awful lot of abuse—verbal and otherwise. And I remember what it would do to the rest of the team. One day, when the other team was 14–0 ahead with three minutes to go in the first half, the players started on Burgie. By the half it was 14–14 and we won the game 43–14. And I know that the way they treated Burghardt really inspired us.

In another game, Burgie and the fellow opposite him were having a blood battle. Burgie had a bad knee, and the fellow knew it. The things this fellow was saying to him—and being right there beside him at guard, I heard every bit of it.

Looking across the huddle at Burgie and seeing his lip bleeding from where he was biting at it, some of our guys wanted to get at this guy. But Burgie said, "This is my fight." There was nothing dirty done, but Burgie literally beat this guy into the ground, just with legitimate football. And in the fourth quarter, they took this fellow out, and he started off the field, and he was wobbling. Then all of a sudden he stopped, turned and came back—I have trouble telling this. He elbowed his way through the two teams, to where we were standing, waiting for play to resume. Tears were running down his face, and he stuck out this hand and he said, "I just want you to know—you're the whitest guy I ever met."

And I thought, that was a lesson that was learned in football.

Daniel "Chappie" James Jr. was the first black four-star general in the United States Air Force. On being promoted to that grade on September 1, 1975, he was assigned as Commander in Chief, North American Air Defense and Aerospace Defense Command, and served in that position until his retirement on February 1, 1978. He died 24 days later.

General James
April 3, 1978

We've had some ugly times in this melting pot we call America but every once in a while we're reminded of a capacity we have for greatness.

Several weeks ago the salutes were fired, the bugles sounded taps and a four star general of the U.S. Air Force was laid to rest in Arlington cemetery. He lies in that place we've set aside for heroes and it is fitting that he should be there for none has deserved it more.

General Daniel "Chappie" James Jr. is younger than many of his rank who rest on those Virginia hills; 58 years old when his great heart gave out. That fine columnist Pat Buchanan wrote in a tribute to General James; "There is the bravery of the soldier in battle, and the man against the mob. There is the moral courage of the individual swimming against the tide of contemporary dogma." Pat has eloquently summed up the heroism of "Chappie" James.

I'm sorry to say I never had an opportunity to meet the General face to face although we talked on the phone a number of times. He was in charge of the homecoming arrangements five years ago for those other heroes—our returning POWs. It was during that period that as Governor we talked to each other by phone as those men returned from Vietnam by way of California.

It was in one of those calls that for some reason he felt it was necessary to tell me he was black. I was surprised—not that he was black—I was well aware of that and told him so trying hard not to add—"so what." My surprise was that he felt he had to interject that in the discussion we were having which was about the flood of requests we were both getting for appearances by the POWs.

I wondered if he felt he had to tell me because he thought

it might make a difference to me. Now thanks to Pat Buchanan I know better. Chappie James the 17th child in his family grew up near Pensacola, Florida in an America that had not awakened to the fact it had a racial problem—a problem he would do something about in his own way.

As a boy military pilots at a nearby base would give him airplane rides in return for chores he did for them. At Tuskegee Institute in Alabama it was only natural that he signed up with the all black cadet unit that became the famed 99th pursuit squadron in World War II. He became an officer but stayed a first lieutenant for seven years. It was unfair but he didn't complain. He flew more than 100 missions in Korea earning almost that many decorations. In Vietnam he was teamed with Colonel Robin Olds. They became famous as "Blackman and Robin"—a take-off on the then current "Batman" TV show. He came home a general and took on campus radicals and protestors in defense of this nation.

He became a four star general joining that exclusive club which includes Ulysses S. Grant and John J. Pershing. He had known times when he was not allowed to enter an officers' club. That didn't make him bitter. He was able to see past that to the real greatness of this land. His photo as a fighter pilot hangs in the Pentagon and on it he has written; "I fought in three wars and three more would not be too many to defend my country. I love America and as she has weaknesses or ills I'll hold her hand."

A Policeman

January 19, 1979

Every once in a while I take the 20 minute flight from Los Angeles to San Diego—usually to address a convention of one kind or another. I always enjoy the visit; San Diego is a beautiful part of our California southland.

I made such a trip recently and while the beauty was unchanged one thing was sadly different. A familiar face was missing at plane side when I came down the ramp. Officer Gene Spurlock of the San Diego police was not on hand. He had been laid to rest the day before my visit.

Gene became a policeman in 1966 at age 29. In all the years I was governor he would be one of those on hand whenever I visited San Diego. For a long time I didn't know he always asked for the assignment. I was very proud when I found that out.

A former high school athlete in San Diego (he still holds the Lincoln High School broad jump record) Gene insisted on serving in the rundown southeast part of the city where he was born. He became the most decorated officer on the force but he was much more than that. Probably no man on the force has ever been more loved and respected by his fellow officers. He was also loved, respected and totally trusted by the people in the district he served.

At his memorial services the police chaplain said: "His ability to bridge the chasm between races and between all people was uncanny. He had what could be called a 'natural knowing' in handling delicate matters involving tensions between the races. He had the ability to create a trust whether arresting them or giving them the last five bucks he had in his pocket." Another tribute came from Mama Williams, a black woman of great dignity who'd had her share of troubles. She said: "He was my friend. How many people can say they had one?" Her seven year old grandson said: "He gave me my nickname 'Tiger'—just say he was my friend."

He believed in justice, he would tear the town apart to clear someone he believed was wrongly accused. Sometimes he paid the bail for the very individuals he had arrested.

About five years ago he was attacked by a painful disease, Reiters syndrome, still he refused to take a less demanding assignment. He stayed with his people, in his neighborhood.

Gene met his wife Betty Lou when they were in 6th grade, he married her when they were in 12th grade. Betty tells how their home was open house on weekends. Black, Brown and White, "his people" would gather just to talk or to have him fix their cars—he was good at that. It was only when his illness grew serious that anyone knew he'd been caring for several needy families for years.

He and Betty knew a great love for 24 years. They have a fine son and two lovely daughters. Gene Spurlock was a legend in the force he was proud to serve. He was 42 years old.

America

Reagan's writings reflect qualities of both Tocqueville and Twain. He was an observer and an advocate. He loved his country and reported stories that he thought illustrated America's uniqueness among nations.

A young man traveled across the land and debunked some myths about the way Americans live.

Long Walk
February 13, 1979

I'm indebted to a columnist in a movie trade paper, "The Hollywood Reporter" for today's commentary. George Christy wrote of an amazing book—*A Walk Across America*—and the young man who did the walking and the writing of the book.

Reagan revered the Oval Office, never using it without wearing a shirt and tie and a suit coat or jacket. But whenever he felt it appropriate he opted for the open neck style of California.

In October 1973, 22 year old Peter Jenkins left his home in Connecticut and started a backpacking trip across America. This was no hike to get from one ocean to the other, or to see how quickly it could be done. The hike ended five years later in Oregon when he waded out waist deep into the Pacific Ocean.

When Peter left Connecticut he didn't think he'd discover America—he thought he knew America and he didn't like it. He was ashamed of the American flag and he didn't believe in God. Peter Jenkins was one of the youthful rebels from the Woodstock era, convinced that Whites in the South hated Blacks and Blacks were all barefoot. He was sure he'd confirm this as he headed south.

He arrived in Murphy, North Carolina flat broke on a Friday night. There was no point in looking for work on a Friday night so he joined a group of black youths who were playing basketball. When the game broke up some of them invited him to their home for dinner. He was afraid but he went. He shared corn bread and fried chicken and spread his bedroll in their yard.

Continuing on he decided Mobile, Alabama was the most beautiful city he'd ever seen. He fell in love with the way of life on the gulf coast and wanted to live there. He discovered the pleasure of a Louisiana "shrimp boil," where he waded with his hosts into the bayou for shrimp and helped with the cooking pots. In Texas he saw the children of oil millionaires and of workers happily going to school together and no way to tell them apart.

Zigzagging across country, moving north as spring came he herded, wrestled, and dehorned cattle. Somewhere in the five years of hiking this young rebel who had vowed marriage was not for him, that he would find and leave girls as it suited him, met and married Barbara. It's all in the book.

Marriage wasn't the only thing he changed his mind about. He describes his walk as a pilgrimage in search of himself. But he found America and he found God. He writes: "Finally I've come around to enjoying being an American. I appreciate being able to go to the grocery store to buy what I want, fish and hunt. I want to become involved with the operation of our schools and government. We often overlook the fact that everyone has an opportunity to have his own home, to create his own world here."

Last Christmas he and Barbara sent out Christmas cards inviting everyone they'd met on the trek to join them for the last mile in Oregon. Over 150 came, ranchers from Idaho, oil men from Texas, the black family from Murphy North Carolina, his and Barbara's families. They waded out waist deep in the ocean, laughing, crying, and embracing.

In his book *A Walk Across America*, he sums it up, "there *is* great love and wonder and hope here, and you're free to pursue your dreams."

Our Country
January 9, 1978

Abraham Lincoln said "a man can disagree with those in government without being against his country or its government."

I have disagreed with those in government on many of these broadcasts. I'm sure I will continue to do so. But just to keep the record straight let me make plain my criticism is not directed against this system of ours which is unique in all the world. I criticize those I believe are turning away from and repudiating the very principles which brought us greatness, eroding individual freedom, robbing us of independence and the right to control our own destiny.

I thought of this the other day when I read an account of a meeting to launch an Australian visitor here on a three month tour of campus appearances. The visitor is hardly a typical representative of the land down under. He has been identified as a collaborator with our enemies in two wars, Korea and Vietnam. A Russian defector claims he has been a Soviet KGB agent. He is telling our college students what is wrong with America and his message is not just a complaint about bureaucratic ineptness. According to him our enemies are the white knights and we are the dragons who must be slain before we devour all that is good and noble in the world.

Well I offer in rebuttal the words spoken a few years ago (when we were still involved in the Vietnam war) by a widely known and respected Canadian commentator who became angry at the rest of the world for, as he put it, kicking us when we were down.

God bless him. Gordon Sinclair went on the radio and said, "It is time to speak up for the Americans as the most generous and possibly the least appreciated people in all the earth."

Then he went on to say: "As long as sixty years ago, when I first started to read newspapers, I read of floods on the Yellow River and the Yangtze. Who rushed in with men and money to help? The Americans did. Germany, Japan and even to a lesser extent Britain and Italy were literally lifted out of the debris of war by the Americans who poured in billions of dollars in aid and forgave other billions in debts. When the franc looked to be in danger of collapsing in 1956 it was the Americans again who propped it up.

"When distant cities are hit by earthquake it is the United States that hurries in to help—Managua, Nicaragua is one of the most recent examples.

"The Marshall plan, the Truman policy, all pumped billions upon billions of dollars into discouraged countries. Now newspapers in those countries are writing about the decadent war mongering Americans.

"I can name you 5,000 times when the Americans raced to the help of other people in trouble. Can you name me even one time when someone else raced to help when the Americans were in trouble." Mr. Sinclair said he wouldn't blame us if we thumbed our nose at the rest of the world. I'm grateful to him but I hope there'll be no nose thumbing. I hope we'll keep right on being the first to arrive when help is needed.

Great nations have fallen in the past, and thus, Reagan says, Americans should not take their country for granted. He urges Americans to be ever vigilant about tending and preserving their nation.

History
August 7, 1978

A few years ago a gentleman named Gary Rekstad wrote a capsulized summary of history under the title, "Once There Was a Great Nation." I've capsulized it even more to fit our time limitation. I thought you'd like to hear it.

Once there was a great nation—"founded by pilgrims who decided to leave their own country which didn't encourage freedom of religion. They migrated to an uncivilized land inhabited only by savages. The rock where they landed was to become a national shrine.

They drove off the natives, built rude shelters and houses of worship, setting aside a special day to give thanks.

These pilgrims believed in their God and they also believed in work. They established schools that in a way became the first public, free education in the world.

Other colonists came and established other communities.

Radio History

It has been said that those who do not heed
the lessons of history are doomed to repeat it.

I'll be right back.

A few years ago a gentleman named Gary Rebated
wrote a capsulized summary of history under the title,
"Once there was a great nation." I've capsulized it even more
to fit our time limitation. I thought you'd like to hear it.

"Once there was a great nation" founded by pilgrims
who decided to leave their own country, which didn't encourage
freedom of religion. They migrated to an uncivilized land
inhabited only by savages. The rock where they landed was
to become a national shrine.

They drove off the natives, built rude shelters & houses of
worship, setting aside a special day to give thanks.

These pilgrims believed in their God & they also believed
in work. They established schools that in a way became the
first public, free ed. in the world.

Other colonists came & established other communities. And
some of the noblest words ever written began to surface. Facades
of our modern bldgs. bear some of them, "liberty," "justice," "freedom
of worship."

Then an older nation sent tax agents to exploit the
colonists. The colonists sent their greatest men as representatives to a
general assembly, choosing a gentleman farmer as their leader.
He united them & won the war against the "Old world." That
farmer is known as the "father of his country." Today a famous
U.S. city is named after him.

Ultimately, a civil war divided the fledgling
country. Its leader who tried to keep the "folks" United was
assassinated. His murder has been immortalized by one of the
greatest playwrights of all time. After the wounds of the bloody
civil war healed, the nation became a world power.

Next the citizens began to think of security paid for by
tax money. Farmers petitioned for price supports. The govt. bought
up crops & stored them in warehouses. Industrialists were next

to ask for tax benefits. The middle class declined 2 under the added tax burden. Crime became so commonplace it was dangerous to walk the streets at night.

A crippled man led the nation into a war and foreign entanglements.

A general who had been victimized by govt. pleaded with the nation to return to the principles of the Founding Fathers. He died bitterly thinking his anguished thoughts.

An honest senator dared to speak out for a halt to foreign aid & foreign subversion. He was branded a reactionary.

The nation fell deeper into debt. It joined a league of the world. Increased taxes to send wheat to its enemies, devalued its currency, substituting base materials for silver in its coins.

That nation's name? Ancient Rome. ~~I should not lengthen this list~~ I skipped a couple of lines to tell you that ~~they~~ (these that) are facts of history. Mr. Rehstad had summed up that the nation—Rome was totally corrupt, its middle class dead. The barbarians moved in and destroyed civilization.

The parallel to our own history is almost eerie, so much so one wonders if we can avoid those last couple of sentences. The rock where those first Romans landed is called the pilgrim rock—foundation of the Temple of Jupiter. The gentleman farmer was ~~Cinc~~ Cincinnatus; The assassinated leader Julius ~~Caesar~~ Caesar; the crippled leader - Caligula; the general Mark Anthony & the honest Senator Cicero. Shakespeare of course the playwright who immortalized the death of Caesar.

How will we finish our story—the story of another great nation?   This is RR. Thanks for listening.

And some of the noblest words ever written began to surface. Facades of our modern buildings bear some of them, 'liberty,' 'justice,' 'freedom of worship.'

Then an older nation sent tax agents to exploit the colonists. The colonists sent their greatest men as representatives to a general assembly, choosing a gentleman farmer as their leader. He united them and won the war against the 'old world.' That farmer is known as the 'father of his country.' Today a famous U.S. city is named after him.

Ultimately, a civil war divided the fledgling country. Its leader who tried to keep the Republic united was assassinated. His murder has been immortalized by one of the greatest playwrights of all time. After the wounds of the bloody civil war healed, the nation became a world power.

Next the citizens began to think of security paid for by tax money. Farmers petitioned for price supports. The government bought up crops and stored them in warehouses. Industrialists were next to ask for tax benefits. The middle class declined under the added tax burden. Crime became so commonplace it was dangerous to walk the streets at night.

A crippled man led the nation into a war and foreign entanglements.

A general who had been victimized by government pleaded with the nation to return to the principles of the founding fathers. He died bitterly thinking his anguished thoughts.

An honest senator dared to speak out for a halt to foreign aid and foreign subversion. He was branded a reactionary.

The nation fell deeper into debt. It joined a league of the world. Increased taxes to send wheat to its enemies, devalued its currency, substituting base materials for silver in its coins."

That nation's name? Ancient Rome. I skipped a couple of lines to tell you that, lines that are facts of history. Mr. Rekstad had summed up that the nation—Rome was totally corrupt, its middle class dead. The barbarians moved in and destroyed civilization.

The parallel to our own history is almost eerie, so much so one wonders if we can avoid those last couple of sentences. The rock where those first Romans landed is called the pilgrim's rock—foundation of the Temple of Jupiter. The gentleman farmer was Cincinnatus; the assassinated leader Julius Caesar; the crippled leader—Caligula; the general Mark Anthony and the honest Senator Cicero. Shakespeare of course the playwright who immortalized the death of Caesar.

How will we finish our story—the story of another great nation?

Amnesty
February 2, 1977

With the pardon of those who not only didn't heed the call of duty but went so far away they couldn't hear it, memories of the Vietnam war pleasant and unpleasant are reawakened. One that came back to me was of an incident so unique it's hard to believe it wasn't considered newsworthy. I can assure you it wasn't, certainly not by the media which found so much immorality in our participation in the war and so little to criticize about Hanoi.

The story has to do with ten separate individuals who fought in Vietnam and returned to this country over a period of about five years. Some were officers, others enlisted men. They had served in the Army, Navy, Marine Corps and Air Force.

Their paths had never crossed in Vietnam. They didn't know each other and upon their return they were scattered all over the United States. They had only one thing in common besides being veterans of the Vietnam war. Each of them was convinced of the rightness of our being there to help the Vietnamese people. Each of them wanted to do more to help.

Ten men in a nation of more than 200 million. What would the odds be against even two of them ever coming together? But they evidently talked about what they felt and what they wished they could do. A listener would hear and say "you ought to know so and so he feels the same way." An address would be given. Two men would correspond. To brief it down eventually these ten men, strangers all, were in touch with each other.

There came a day when they journeyed to Washington. Their request sounded simple—"We are Vietnam veterans who want to do something to help the Vietnamese people before the American withdrawal. Will you send us back?" It sounded simple yes—but it took quite a bit of doing. They were now civilians asking to be sent to a war zone and they finally made it.

Their destination was the village of Cat Lai and they had decided on their mission. They wanted to build houses for disabled Vietnamese veterans. They called themselves the Cat Lai Commune.

Day in, day out they worked. The villagers accepted them and quietly understood. One of the happiest notes in this story is the lack of surprise on the part of the people in Cat Lai. What these ten young men were doing was in keeping with what the Vietnamese had come to believe was typical of Americans.

In the evenings they would sit around in the warm twilight having a beer with the villagers and the disabled men they were trying to help. On one of those evenings they told a young Vietnamese officer that back in America there were many Americans who thought the people of Vietnam would be better off under Hanoi.

He replied, "I think my country is the h—l of the world; you have come to this h—l to help us. We have been at war for thousands of years. We want peace more than anyone but we want peace without communism."

I don't know what finally happened to those ten men or when they came home. But as the planes from Canada and Sweden bring others home I'm going to try and remember the Cat Lai Commune.

During World War II Reagan enlisted in the Army as 2nd Lieutenant and was discharged as Captain in 1945. For years he made special films, ranging from explaining how to tell a Japanese "Zero" from one of our planes to explaining the war effort and building morale.

Vietnam War

May 29, 1979

The Oscar was given on Academy Award night to the motion picture *The Deer Hunter.* I'm sure you all know the movie deals with the Vietnam war. If you haven't seen it then possibly you don't know that it is a story of friendship among young men; that it certainly does not glorify war although it is unashamedly patriotic and it doesn't call down punishment on the United States for being in that war.

It is this last point that has caused some to withhold congratulations for its award of the Oscar. Those who in the 1960s and early '70s saw no virtue in anything America did, and only nobility of purpose on the part of North Vietnam, cannot of course accept any story about that war which doesn't follow that theme.

Indeed they can't accept the truth let alone a fictional version. I wish someone in the world of TV or the movies would do a film about the men who endured captivity for 6, 8 and 10 years in the Hanoi Hilton as it was called or any of the other Communist torture camps.

Capt. John McCain, U.S. Navy, spent six years in the hands of the North Vietnamese. One day he was told he was to meet an "American actress" who was for peace. Recognizing a propaganda trick, he refused. He was beaten, starved, finally put in an unventilated box five feet long and two feet wide and kept there for four steaming summer months.

If the producing gentry in Hollywood want to follow up on *The Deer Hunter*'s success there is plenty of material at hand. Scott Blakey has written a book called *Prisoner At War—The Survival of Commander Richard A. Stratton*. It's published by Anchor Press/Doubleday.

Dick Stratton was a prisoner more than six years. His story is one of love as well as war; of a wife who never lost hope. And it is the story of dozens if not hundreds of the men who were his fellow prisoners. There are amazing tales revealed for the first time. One such concerns Admiral Jeremiah Denton.

If you remember that long night when we all watched TV waiting for the landing at Clark Field in the Philippines of that first plane bringing our POWs home, Jeremiah Denton was the first man we saw. He made his way down the ramp, saluted the flag, and thanked us for bringing them home.

You might not remember that you had seen him a few years before on TV when his captors forced him through torture to be filmed telling us how well they were all being treated. He stood there before the microphone his eyes blinking in the harsh TV lights. But now thanks to Scott Blakey's book we know it wasn't the lights that made him blink. He was spelling out in Morse Code the word "tortured" over and over again.

When the film was played on network TV in America a Naval Intelligence officer recognized and read the message.

Naturally this had to be kept secret while our men were still prisoners.

You'll learn a lot from the book and you'll get a little impatient with those who don't like pictures that don't hate America.

People

REAGAN RARELY SPOKE OF THE "PUBLIC" AND NEVER OF THE "MASSES." INSTEAD HE VIEWED PEOPLE AS FASCINATING INDIVIDUALS, EACH WITH HIS OR HER OWN VIRTUES AND FAULTS. IN THE NEXT FOUR STORIES HE TELLS OF SOME SPECIAL VIRTUES, ESPECIALLY COURAGE.

This story is about a young female student at the University of California at San Diego who, in the middle of the anti-Vietnam war demonstrations during Reagan's governorship, stepped forward to shake his hand, braving the contempt of many of her peers. She spoke twelve words that he never forgot.

"Sometimes, big international meetings can get dull. At a summit of the leaders of the world's democracies, someone was droning on, and Ronald Reagan was bored. I looked over and he was making drawings on his notepad. When the meeting was over, he got up to leave. I asked, 'Mr. President, are you through with your notepad?' He said, 'Yes.' 'May I have it?' 'Yes.' 'Would you sign?' He signed."—George P. Shultz

Missing Person
April 3, 1978

Having had intimate contact with some of the most violent of our universities during the days of anti-war and anti-almost anything demonstrations it's a joy to be invited to a campus today. The students are courteous to visitors, aware of world happenings, and have inquiring not closed minds.

The contrast aroused many memories of that different time a decade ago and one experience in particular I'd like to share with you. As Governor I was automatically a member of the Board of Regents of the University of California. The board met monthly, rotating the meeting place to each of the nine campuses.

As the governing body of the university the board was of course a legitimate target for the dissidents. Some would even travel from their own campus to the meeting place to make sure we would receive a proper reception.

The incident that continues to haunt me occurred on the campus at San Diego. I arrived there on one of those grey California mornings. Any place else you'd say it was a cloudy day. In California it is a high fog but it still makes for a dreary day. It wasn't brightened any when the advance security detail told me a special reception had been planned for my arrival.

It seems the meeting was being held in a building deep in the campus requiring about a 200 yard walk. The demonstrators had decided on a kind of silent vigil. The walk to the entrance of the building was flanked by grass covered sloping embankments on which the students had gathered several deep leaving only a narrow path through which I would have to march while they stared silently down at me.

Security had another idea not knowing whether the vigil would remain silent (and inactive) for the whole 200 yard walk. They said they could drive me to the rear of the building and smuggle me in through a back door.

Frankly I'd had it by this time with the riots, the pickets and the vandalism and I refused. Their silent vigil wasn't going to keep me from going in the front door. So I started down the narrow path.

It's pretty hard not to appear self conscious with more than a thousand hostile young people—most of them almost near enough to touch watching your every step and expression. It was a long 200 yards.

I was almost to the end of the ordeal when a rather small, attractive, blonde girl stepped out of the crowd and stood on the walk facing me. I thought "Oh Dear Lord what have they planned for me now." But she put out her hand and spoke, her voice ringing like a bell in all that deep silence. She said "I just want to tell you I like everything you are doing." I took her hand but I couldn't thank her, there was a baseball-size lump in my throat.

I've never forgotten that moment and her courage. I could go on into the building; she had to stay out there with her peers. I never found out who she was. How I wish I could. I'd like to tell her what her bravery meant to me. I'd like to say thanks.

President Calvin Coolidge, derided by many historians, was one of Reagan's favorites. One of the first things Reagan did after he became president was to hang Coolidge's portrait in a place of honor in the Roosevelt Room in the West Wing of the White House. This story explains why.

President Coolidge
September 21, 1976

The names of some presidents are invoked by spokesmen of both political parties as "men for all seasons," epitomizing the greatness of America, Washington, Lincoln, Jefferson, etc. Then there are presidents whose names are brought up in party circles, hailed as great but if acknowledged by the other party at all with not quite the same enthusiasm.

There are also two lists of presidential names—one for each party usually held up to view for strictly partisan purposes. Each party lists past presidents of the opposing party as examples of that party's terrible record.

The Democrats for example get laughs by mentioning silent Cal Coolidge. And truth is many Republicans chuckle a little and go along with the idea that he was a do nothing president. Sometimes I wonder if he really was a "do nothing" or was he a little like a lifeguard on the beach who also seems to be doing very little when there is no emergency. If you take a closer look he is quietly being watchful.

Cal Coolidge is good for laughs but not all of them are at his expense. There was the press conference where a persistent reporter asked the President if he had anything to say about Prohibition. Cal said "No."—"Any comments on the world court?"—"No." "What about the farm situation?" Again the answer was "No." The reporter said, "You don't seem to have any comment about anything." Coolidge said, "No comment and don't quote me."

Probably no president has ever lived in the White House and maintained so unchanged his previous lifestyle. Which in Coolidge's case was the simple even frugal life he had lived on a New England farm.

Shortly after he became president he sent his teenage son into the tobacco fields to work in the summer as he always had. One of the other workers surprised at this said to the young Coolidge, "If my father were president I wouldn't be out here working in the field." Young Coolidge said, "If my father were your father you would."

But while "Silent Cal" seemed to be doing nothing as President, the federal budget actually went down and so did the national debt. Consumer prices fell but unemployment stayed at the figure we only dream of—$3\frac{1}{2}$ percent, which means everyone who wanted a job had one. Federal taxes were cut four times.

Right now we are all concerned with
who will be our ~~future~~ Pres. For whatever it's
worth I'm going to talk about a Pres. from the past.
I'll be right back.

The names of some Presidents are invoked by
spokesmen of both pol. parties as "men for all seasons,"
~~typical~~ epitomizing the greatness of America, Washington,
Lincoln, Jefferson etc. Then there are Presidents whose
names are brought up in party circles, hailed as
great but if ~~any~~ acknowledged by the other party ~~at all~~
with quite the same enthusiasm.

There are two lists of Presidential names — one
for each party ~~regularly held up to view~~ for strictly
partisan purposes. Each party lists past Presidents
of the opposing party as examples of that parties
terrible record. ~~terrible~~

The Demos. for example get laughs by mentioning
Silent Cal Coolidge. And truth is many Repubs. chuckle
a little and go along with the idea that he was
a do nothing Pres. Sometimes I wonder if he really
was a "do nothing" or was he a little like a Life Guard
on the beach who also seems to be doing very little
when there is no emergency. If you take a closer
look he is quietly being watchful.

Cal Coolidge ~~was~~ is good for laughs but not
all of them are at his expense. There ~~was~~ The ~~press~~
~~conference~~ press conference where a persistent reporter asked
the Pres. if he had anything to ~~say~~ about prohibition? Cal said
"No." — "Any comment as the world court?" — "No." "What
about the farm situation? Again the ans. was "no." The
reporter said, "You don't seem to have any comment about
anything." Coolidge said, "No comment & don't quote me."

Probably no Pres. has ever lived in the White House
and maintained so unchanged his previous life style.

2

Which in Coolidge case was the simple even frugal life he had lived on a New England farm.

Shortly after he became Pres. he sent his teen age son into the tobacco fields to work in the summer as he always had. One of the other workers surprised at this said to the young Coolidge, "if my father were Pres. I wouldn't be out here working in the field." Young Coolidge said, "If my father were your father, you would."

But while "Silent Cal" seemed to be doing nothing as Pres. the Fed. budget actually went down & so did the Nat'l debt. Consumer prices fell but unemp. stayed at the figure we only dream of – 3½% which means everyone who wanted a job had one. Fed. taxes were cut 4 times.

The number of automobiles on our streets & highways tripled during his years in the White House and radio sales went up 1400%.

In fact the 5 years from 1922 to 27 the purchasing power of wages rose 10%. It was a kind of "Golden era" in the ways. ~~in its instrument and & in the sports arena~~. Hollywood would never again be more glamorous and there were giants in the sports arenas whose names are still ~~from a~~ legend – The Manassa Mauler, Jack Dempsey, Knute Rockne, The 4 Horsemen, Red Grange, Babe Ruth & Big Bill Tilden. Now I'm not saying Pres. Coolidge was responsible for them but they were larger than life figures that went with Americas place in the world. ~~I often Cal Coolidge was a do nothing Pres.~~

So what if he was a "do nothing" Pres. Do you suppose doing nothing had ~~something~~ SOMETHING to do with ~~balancing budget~~, reducing the debt & cutting taxes 4 times? This is R.R.

Thanks for listening.

The number of automobiles on our streets and highways tripled during his years in the White House and radio sales went up 1400 percent.

In just the five years from 1922 to 1927 the purchasing power of wages rose 10 percent. It was a kind of Golden Era, in other ways. Hollywood would never again be more glamorous and there were giants in the sports arenas whose names are still legend—the Manassa Mauler, Jack Dempsey, Knute Rockne, The Four Horsemen, Red Grange, Babe Ruth and Big Bill Tilden. Now I'm not saying President Coolidge was responsible for them but they were larger than life figures that went with America's place in the world

So what if he was a "do nothing" president. Do you suppose doing nothing had something to do with reducing the budget, reducing the debt and cutting taxes four times?

Television
January 19, 1977

What does a symphony orchestra musician, a good car mechanic and a maker of fine sauces have in common? Plenty if they are all the same fellow.

Not too long ago on this program I was critical of the news media, particularly the TV news programs plus a few talk shows for what I called an anti-business attitude. In fact while admitting I couldn't claim to have seen all the shows, I said I couldn't recall ever seeing any advocates of free enterprise holding forth on TV.

Well now I can! T'was the night after Christmas and there on the set was a story that proved we have a good bet. Forgive me for that it's the season. I was watching CBS News and if you were, you saw a story about one of our fellow citizens who hadn't done any of the things for which a person usually winds up in the headlines.

A goodly portion of the evening news was devoted to this 45-year-old man, father of four, son of an immigrant father. None of that is what you might call earthshaking or even newsworthy. There isn't a headline in the fact that he was a high school dropout or even that he served in the Army. Too many Americans have done both.

But to its credit CBS News did a heartwarming story about this resident of one of our eastern cities. First of all he didn't settle for being a dropout. He took advantage of the educational opportunities the military offered and wound up with a college degree.

He and his brother have an auto repair shop and they are the repairmen. He also has a talent in the kitchen which he has used to good advantage. In the evenings he cooks sauces for spaghetti, shrimp, and so forth. His family helps and they package and sell the product to markets and other outlets.

There are however some evenings when he isn't in the kitchen. He plays in the city's philharmonic orchestra and you can't do that without putting in a fair share of time at rehearsal.

I hope I haven't given the impression that this American

citizen is just a terribly energetic, ambitious fellow moonlighting and driving himself round the clock to keep up with the Joneses and the cost of living. No the subject of the CBS News special places a great importance on living. He enjoys what he's doing.

Some way he's found time to develop an appreciation of fine wine, join a wine tasting society and accumulate knowledge to match his appreciation. A number of people aspiring to the same appreciation call on our citizen for help in acquiring the knowledge to go with it.

Before that CBS News special feature ended this American citizen told the rest of us how much opportunity there is in this land—in this way of life we call America. And he made it very clear he wasn't just touting the Babbitt line of how to make a buck. He was talking about living and he made us realize he truly enjoyed his life and everything he was doing. And he made us realize the same joy is available to anyone who'll take advantage of being an American. The last we saw of him he was putting the finishing touches on a fender in the auto repair shop. Thank you CBS News.

This is the story of a 27-year-old man, crippled by an accident so he will never again walk, who struggles to work out a way to overcome his handicap. It is an example of what touched Reagan deeply and how, in his own way, he tried to help.

Horse and Rider I
November 28, 1978

Anne Keegan, writing in the *Chicago Tribune* on November 3rd, is the source of today's commentary. She wrote of a husky young man (age 27) who worked on an Illinois river barge until one day a two inch metal cable broke. As it snapped back it whipped around his body like a boa constrictor, crushing his lower spine. Jim Hendricks became a paraplegic. That was four years ago.

After a period of feeling sorry for himself (which I'm sure we can all understand) he made up his mind that he wouldn't settle for growing old in a wheel chair doing nothing.

Jim had been raised around horses all his life and his first love had been riding. He decided he was going to ride again. You know there is an old cavalry saying that nothing is so good for the inside of a man as the outside of a horse. I don't know whether Jim was familiar with that saying, but he knew riding would make him, as he put it, feel human again.

First, of course, he needed a horse—a big boned, stocky, quiet horse with common sense and intelligence. He found his mount, standing in a pasture, unbroken as yet. But that was all right because he would have to be trained in a special way.

Borrowing money from the bank to buy the horse, a truck to haul him and some left over to pay for training, he put up his mobile home as collateral. Then he went hunting for a trainer. A special kind of trainer who could teach a horse to lie down so Jim could get aboard and then get up carrying his rider.

He found his man—an old trick rider—now blind.

Bud Jones was more than a little doubtful about the project but when he saw how determined Jim was he gave it a try. It was a good try and Calvin—that's what Jim named his horse—learned in three months what they thought would take a year.

Jim and Calvin became close friends and Calvin seemed to sense the need to take care of his friend. He learned a number of tricks. Jim made himself a leg brace and, with crutches, could stand and move around just a little. But he rode without any straps or safety devices.

Then one day Bud suggested that Jim and Calvin should do the horse show circuit and perhaps some county fairs. Jim said no at first, but when Bud pointed out it might be helpful and inspiring to others with handicaps he went on the road billed as "Hopalong, the World's Only Paraplegic Trick Rider and His Horse Calvin." They did rodeos, fairs and just about anything that would take them. When people would marvel at Jim's ability to ride, he'd give the credit to Calvin.

It would be nice if the story of Jim Hendricks, paraplegic,

Reagan was always happy when he got to his ranch, but he was happiest when he slid into the saddle on one of his favorite horses. As he often said, "Nothing is so good for the inside of a man as the outside of a horse."

blind Bud Jones and Calvin ended right here, but unfortunately there is more. I'll tell you about it in the next broadcast.

Horse and Rider II
November 28, 1978

On the last broadcast I told of how Jim Hendricks a paraplegic as the result of an accident decided to take up horseback riding. He mortgaged his mobile home to buy an unbroken horse and truck to haul his horse. He found an ex-trick rider now blind who taught his unbroken horse to lie down so he could be mounted and to do a number of tricks.

Then Jim and his horse Calvin went out on the circuit, playing rodeos, horse shows and fairs. They received a fee but actually only broke even what with feed bills and hire of an assistant at each stop. In fact Jim never took a motel or hotel room but slept in the stable with Calvin. But they were having fun and life had a purpose. His support was from Social Security disability out of which he paid the installments on his mortgage.

Then last August Jim and Calvin came in off the road and found his disability had been cut off because he had missed a medical re-examination. He was told he'd have to appeal the decision and that would take three or four months. But then they added that even if he won the appeal and was declared medically eligible he still wouldn't get any checks because he'd become a performer. They turned a deaf ear when he explained he didn't actually make any money—that he was doing it to encourage other handicapped people.

Finally the bank notified him that unless he could resume payments on his loan they'd have to take his mobile home, his truck and Calvin. Trainer Bud Jones says that would probably mean the slaughterhouse for Calvin because he won't let anyone but Jim ride him. Others have tried and been thrown. Calvin seems to be more understanding than the people at Social Security. He has a sixth sense about his handicapped owner and takes care of him.

Jim has begged the bank to take his trailer and his truck but not Calvin. He says; "I'd lay down my life for that horse. He's everything to me. He's my pleasure and my protector. He's given me a purpose in life since my accident." Jim feels his back is to the wall. If his disability isn't restored there is no way that he and Calvin can go on. As he puts it: "I'm the type I don't worry if it's just a can of beans on the table for supper. So they can come and take everything to my name. But I don't know how I'll get along if they come and take my best friend away."

Anyone who rides knows how Jim Hendricks of Pleasantview, Illinois feels. Social Security computers can't know nor apparently can any of those desk jockeys who live by the book. I wonder how many discouraged and depressed people with handicaps have been encouraged to find a purpose in life after seeing Jim Hendricks as "Hopalong, the World's only Paraplegic Cowboy and His Horse Calvin"?

Values and Virtues

THE FIRST STORY IN THIS SECTION REFLECTS REA-
GAN'S BASIC VIEW ON VALUES. IN THE OTHERS HE
FINDS VALUES AND VIRTUES EXPRESSED THROUGH IN-
DIVIDUAL ACTS OF GENEROSITY, COURAGE, COMMIT-
MENT, AND GOODNESS.

Do Right
February 20, 1978

Every generation thinks the preceding generation left the world in a mess for them to straighten out. Each generation challenges the mores and customs of the past. We did it, our parents before us did it and our children's children will do it. There's nothing wrong with that as long as some generation doesn't discard time tested, proven values simply because they are old.

Charles Edison, son of the great genius Thomas Edison has written something I thought you might like to hear. He tells that a reporter once asked his father if he had any "advice for youth." Thomas Edison replied: "Youth never takes advice" and went about his business. Then Charles writes:

Like my father, I doubt that my advice will be taken. Youth seems to like to learn the hard way—on the battlefield of their own experience. However, here are some thoughts derived from my travels through seventy-three years of life.

My "advice" is double edged: it is presented to youth and, by the same token, to our country. For our country and its youth are synonymous. My generation—and the generation immediately preceding it—will soon be a memory—either pleasant or unpleasant, depending on the effect our lives had on our country. It is you—the young people of America—who will be taking over.

The basic ingredient of my advice is a resurrection of honor. Honor, an old-fashioned word, but one that encompasses everything—duty, responsibility, knowledge and adherence to one's heritage and traditions, respect for the eternal values. An honorable man can live a life free from fear. He knows his duties to his family, his

Each generation ~~challenges the mores & customs of~~
~~the past and that's as it should be so long as youth~~
~~don't discard proven values simply because they are old.~~
~~It's been going along fine~~

It's nice to think that maybe ~~things~~ the younger
generation doesn't have any faults that becoming a
parent & a taxpayer won't cure. I'll be right back.

Every generation thinks the preceding generation
left the world in a mess for them to straighten out.
Each generation challenges the mores & customs of the
past. We did it, our parents before us did it & our
children's children will do it. There's nothing wrong
with that as long as ~~one does~~ some generation doesn't discard
time tested, proven values simply because they are old.

Charles Edison, son of the great genius Thomas
Edison has written something I thought you might like
to hear. He tells that a reporter once asked his
father if he had any "advice for youth". Thomas Edison
replied: "youth never takes advice" & went about his
business. Then Charles writes:

~~Charles writes:~~

~~*Do Right*~~

~~Many years ago, a reporter asked my father whether he had any "advice for youth." My father answered: "Youth never takes advice" and went about his business.~~

Like my father, I doubt that my advice will be taken. Youth seems to like to learn the hard way—on the battlefield of their own experience. However, here are some thoughts derived from my travels through seventy-three years of life.

My "advice" is double edged: it is presented to youth and, by the same token, to our country. For our country and its youth are synonymous. My generation—and the generation immediately preceding it—will soon be a memory—either pleasant or unpleasant, depending on the effect our lives had on our country. It is you—the young people of America—who will be taking over.

The basic ingredient of my advice is a resurrection of honor. Honor, an old-fashioned word, but one that encompasses everything—duty, responsibility, knowledge and adherence to one's heritage and traditions, respect for the eternal values. An honorable man can live a life free from fear. He knows his duties to his family, his community and his nation, and will exercise them to the best of his ability. He is aware of his responsibilities—first to himself and then to the world around him. He takes the trouble to learn his background—his family, his nation and his God—and uses this knowledge to enrich his own life and the life of all around him. The honorable man cherishes the heritage made available to him by his family, by the founding fathers of his nation and by the thousands of years of history in which men strove for freedom and decency. He knows and respects the eternal values which have come to him from all these years and from all these peoples. A man's honor is the greatest treasure he owns. It will make him rich beyond all dreams of avarice.

And so, the essence of my advice is to seek out the meaning of honor and, once this is realized, to exercise honor as the basic force of life. //

~~"When in doubt—do right."~~

→ Then Charles Edison sums it all up in this infallible guideline for individuals & for ~~great~~ governments.

" When in doubt — do right."

This RR Thanks for listening.

community and his nation, and will exercise them to the best of his ability. He is aware of his responsibilities—first to himself and then to the world around him. He takes the trouble to learn his background—his family, his nation and his God—and uses this knowledge to enrich his own life and the life of all around him. The honorable man cherishes the heritage made available to him by his family, by the founding fathers of his nation and by the thousands of years of history in which men strove for freedom and decency. He knows and respects the eternal values which have come to him from all these years and from all these peoples. A man's honor is the greatest treasure he owns. It will make him rich beyond all dreams of avarice.

And so, the essence of my advice is to seek out the meaning of honor and, once this is realized, to exercise honor as the basic force of life.

Then Charles Edison sums it all up in this infallible guideline for individuals and for governments. "When in doubt—do right."

Lawrence Welk
February 13, 1979

As our country was approaching its bicentennial, a man wrote a book called *My America, Your America*. In the foreword he says, "I know that this wonderful life of mine could never have happened anywhere but here. My parents knew this long before me. Searching for freedom, they came to this country as immigrants, from a land where they and their parents before them had been bitterly oppressed—trapped in a life where there was little or no chance to better themselves."

You can see and hear this man any week on TV. Just treat yourself to an hour's entertainment that will (if you're old enough) bring back nostalgic memories of the big band era. There he is, one time farm boy, son of immigrants, telling us, "It's Wunnerful, Wunnerful."

And Lawrence Welk has done something to make life wonderful for those around him. Take a look at his company of more than 50 people and see if you can't feel the genuine warmth and camaraderie of his musicians and artists. You can because it's there.

In this cynical world where too often a broken promise doesn't count unless it was in writing, the Lawrence Welk company operates with no written contracts. This is part of the "Welk Training and Sharing Plan." A great many business executives and industrialists could do themselves a favor by having Lawrence explain his plan to them.

Very simply the plan consists of three parts. Number one is the training program. Young talent is discovered, is trained by the employer and senior employees. The trainees are paid during a training period which does not exceed one year. At the year's end employee and employer review progress and decide whether to continue the relationship. If the decision is yes, the trainee becomes a full employee and begins from

Reagan made over fifty movies, the last one in 1964. As befits one of the top stars in Hollywood, he was a dapper dresser. Notice the cuffs and lapel flower in this movie studio publicity photo.

that day to share in the profits and other benefits of the business.

Part 2 of the plan is a corporation which sets aside an amount equal to 15 percent of the gross payroll. This money is deposited and invested for the sole benefit of the employees. If and when they retire or leave the company they get their share. There are in addition, special benefits and bonuses for meritorious effort. The corporation also assumes all or part of the payment for medical coverage, life insurance, union assessments, etc.

And Part 3 is the no contract basis. As Lawrence explains it: "The prime goal of our job training and sharing program is to develop the individual person to the highest possible degree of his inborn talents and potential in every way—personally, professionally, morally and spiritually. This goal is the basic, underlying motivation for our entire system."

Does the system work? In the back stage life, TV viewers never see there is an unmistakable family spirit. They baby sit for each other, take trips together and help each other in time of trouble. Sounds real American doesn't it? Lawrence Welk's bicentennial book *My America, Your America* should be required reading for all of us. It's wunnerful, wunnerful.

Good News
November 8, 1977

A few weeks ago there was an item on the sport page datelined SEATTLE. It had to do with a couple of well known football players and a young fellow you've never heard of—until now.

The Buffalo Bills were on their way to meet the Seattle Seahawks. The players I referred to are the Bills' great running back O.J. Simpson and Jim Zorn. They had a get acquainted meeting with a young fellow named Jimmy Gallegos. Jimmy is just fourteen and thinks it was quite an honor to meet two pro-stars of the stature of Simpson and Zorn. Somehow I have a feeling that O.J. Simpson and Jim Zorn left the meeting feeling that maybe they were the ones who had been honored.

You see fourteen-year-old Jimmy Gallegos has cancer. In July of 1976 his left arm was amputated at the shoulder—as the doctors put it to buy him some time.

In November of 1976—just a year ago part of one lung was removed. And now he has a tumor in the other lung. The news story said it is sometimes a little hard for him to get going in the morning. His doctor's greatest fear is pneumonia. He had a bout with it last August but came through all right.

Jimmy has a good friend—his counselor at Washington Junior High in Yakima, Jerry Gibbons. It was Gibbons who learned that Jimmy had three wishes—to go deep sea fishing, to see a good football game and to meet O.J. Simpson.

His interest in football—all sports for that matter comes naturally. He is a *starting* player on the Washington Junior High football, basketball and baseball teams.

Yes that's right, this fourteen-year-old who has lost his left arm at the shoulder, who has only one-and-a-half lungs with a tumor in the one, is a regular in three sports. None of this according to Gibbons is honorary. Jimmy Gallegos is a regular player because he's the best player for his position in all three sports.

Last year when his arm was amputated, he was back on the diamond playing baseball one week later. As Jerry Gibbons says "he's a gutsy kid." Jimmy's mother says that, "He considers himself lucky because so much of the time he sees other kids who can't move around or do anything."

It isn't given to us to know or understand God's plan for each one of us—we simply must have faith in his infinite wisdom and mercy knowing that he has a purpose. I think we can be sure of one thing though—the world has to be a little better because there's a gutsy kid named Jimmy Gallegos in Yakima, Washington.

I hope he had a good visit with O.J. Simpson and Jim Zorn. I'm sure they are grateful for the opportunity they had to make one of Jimmy's three wishes come true.

Human Nature, The Economy, and Progress

IN REAGAN'S VIEW, HUMAN NATURE IS THE ENGINE THAT MAKES ECONOMIC AND SOCIAL PROGRESS POSSIBLE. MAN IS MOST CREATIVE AND INNOVATIVE WHEN HE IS UNHAMPERED BY INSTITUTIONAL RESTRAINTS.

Red Hen
November 16, 1976

A modern day little Red Hen may not appear to be a quotable authority on economics but then some authorities on economics aren't worth quoting. This is a little treatise on basic economics called "The Modern Little Red Hen."

Once upon a time there was a little red hen who scratched about the barnyard until she uncovered some grains of wheat.

President Reagan has just been told his large 1981 tax cut has passed the Congress. He cannot resist drawing a sketch of himself smiling—and then posing with it to show how intensely pleased he is. This is probably as close as he ever came to showing off.

She called her neighbors and said, "If we plant this wheat, we shall have bread to eat. Who will help me plant it?"

"Not I," said the cow.

"Not I," said the duck.

"Not I," said the pig.

"Not I," said the goose.

"Then I will," said the little red hen. And she did. The wheat grew tall and ripened into golden grain. "Who will help me reap my wheat?" asked the little red hen.

"Not I," said the duck.

"Out of my classification," said the pig.

"I'd lose my seniority," said the cow.

"I'd lose my unemployment compensation," said the goose.

"Then I will," said the little red hen, and she did.

At last it came time to bake the bread. "Who will help me bake bread?" asked the little red hen.

"That would be overtime for me," said the cow.

"I'd lose my welfare benefits," said the duck.

"I'm a dropout and never learned how," said the pig.

"If I'm to be the only helper, that's discrimination," said the goose.

"Then I will," said the little red hen.

She baked five loaves and held them up for her neighbors to see.

They all wanted some and, in fact, demanded a share. But the little red hen said, "No, I can eat the five loaves myself."

"Excess profits," cried the cow.
"Capitalist leech," screamed the duck.
"I demand equal rights," yelled the goose.
And the pig just grunted.

And they painted "unfair" picket signs and marched round and round the little red hen, shouting obscenities.

When the government agent came, he said to the little red hen,
"You must not be greedy."
"But I earned the bread," said the little red hen.
"Exactly," said the agent. "That is the wonderful free enterprise system. Anyone in the barnyard can earn as much as he wants. But under our modern government regulations, the productive workers must divide their product with the idle."

And they lived happily ever after, including the little red hen, who smiled and clucked, "I am grateful, I am grateful."

But her neighbors wondered why she never baked any more bread.

Socialism
November 30, 1976

My award for someone who thought of the right answer while the discussion was still going on is a young man named

Brad Linaweaver, a member of Young Americans for Freedom at Pennsylvania State University. He has written of an encounter on the campus with a pretty young lady who believes socialism is the answer to our problems.

His own philosophy was self-evident because he was wearing a button that proclaimed "Cut Down Big Government." With the cool breeze stirring her hair she asked what Brad described as her "ace-up-the-sleeve" question, "Even you right wingers don't want to starve. Wouldn't you like a guarantee that you won't ever go hungry?" Brad knew that if he admitted to this she'd follow with why not such a guarantee for shelter, medicine and all the rest.

He paused and then gave her the victory she was seeking—or so she thought. He said, "Sure I'd like to lay my hands on everything I can get." "Ah," she said, "But the state is the closest you can come to such a guarantee." Brad described her as braced for a counter-attack invoking the magic of the "market mechanism." But he threw another curve. "Sure," he said, "I grant that. There's something more. I'd like a guarantee of shelter and medical treatment and even some recreation." She must have thought she had a convert. A little shocked she spoke: "But that's what we support. Why are you wearing that button?" She meant of course that "Cut Down Big Government" button.

Brad wasn't finished, he said to her, "I would also like a yacht." Somewhat deflated she answered—". . . if you're not going to be serious about it." "But I am," Brad said as earnestly as he could. "I would really and truly like a yacht.

Also a seaside villa." "Look," she said sternly "you know what I'm talking about—Sharing! I'm not interested in your greedy daydreams. I'm asking what everyone should have." "All right," Brad answered, "I understand. Let everyone have a yacht."

"But how?" she asked lucidly with the first sign of a rational thought. "Don't bother me with that" he said. "There will be a way, I'm sure. Just so everyone has a yacht. However there is one more thing I would like." "What?" she asked. "Two yachts." Brad wrote she looked rather unpleasant at that point and he feared for his safety. Then she declared, "It's people like you who keep socialism from working."

Brad agreed, "Yes, quite right. Perhaps if people like me were put away somewhere socialism would have a chance." By now she was really glaring as she tried to think of an answer. Brad continued, "But there's still one problem. How many are there like me?" "Not as many as you think," she said and walked away. And then Brad came up with a really appropriate last line. He wrote "There she is wrong. And that's why she is a socialist."

How right he is. Socialists ignore the side of man that is of the spirit. They can provide shelter, fill your belly with bacon and beans, treat you when you are ill, all the things that are guaranteed to a prisoner or a slave. They don't understand that we dream—yes even of some time owning a yacht.

Kettering
September 6, 1977

Our sons and daughters will in their lifetime undoubtedly see things almost impossible for us to imagine. But in my opinion the generation to which I belong will have had an experience they will not know.

There have only been a few periods at most in man's history when a single generation presided over a great transition. Our generation was one of those. We literally went from the horse and buggy to travel in outer space; to the miracles of communication by which you are hearing my voice. But I don't want to sound like that man back in the late 1800s who wanted to close down the U.S. Patent Office because everything had been invented. Nor do I want to sound boastful or smug about the miracles that became commonplace in our lifetime.

Each generation sees farther than the generation that preceded it because we stand on the shoulders of giants.

Back in 1943, when radio had opened a new world to us, General Motors had a great Sunday afternoon program of symphonic music. On October 3rd of that year C.F. Kettering, a GM vice president and director of research, made a short address on radio. He called attention to how much we all owe the generations that preceded us.

Speaking of how radio could carry the music of the orchestra all over the world he said the elements of radio had been developing over 100 years. Then surprisingly this remarkable engineering genius said that in truth the miracle of radio had started 600 years before Christ—2500 years ago.

He made it clear it was only a vague, weak thought at that time when a Greek philosopher Thales of Miletus found that by rubbing amber he produced a force that would pick up straws. Two thousand two hundred years later Queen Elizabeth's physician in England, Sir William Gilbert, did a little playing around with the idea and called the phenomenon he produced, electricity. Sixty years later a German, von Gueriche, built a machine that generated static electricity. A century later Benjamin Franklin identified positive and negative electricity and proved electricity and lightning were one and the same.

Kettering went on in his radio address and told how in 1820 a Dane named Oersted proved that electricity would produce magnetism. The idea was moving faster; Faraday discovered the principle of the electric motor. Morse and Bell came along and used the idea to communicate by way of the telegraph and the telephone. Edison lighted the world with it and Marconi and deForest laid the foundation for radio.

Pointing out how these men, unknowing of each other for the most part, spread and separated over 2500 years brought that vague idea to a force that literally changed the face of the earth, Kettering spoke of how indestructible an idea is. He also said there have only been a few thousand such thought cultivators in all man's history and without them we might still be living in caves.

Mr. Kettering had saved his surprise for the last. He

closed his speech saying, "We might go back 2500 years to 600 BC and find out why the amber picked up the straws. We don't know that yet." And he added, "If we did I believe we could open up new fields that might be quite as important as the electric light, the telephone or the radio."

Pollution #1
August 1975

Memory is far from infallible and when it comes to the "good old days" it leaves out a lot of the not so good.

Not so long ago I found myself in a discussion concerning the state of the world with some young people including my own children. Strangely enough it wasn't old Dad who was nostalgic about the good old days and sour about today's world. No, it was the "now" generation who were pessimistic about where we are and where we're going. They almost seemed resentful toward me because I'd known that other world of yesterday when life was simple and good with joy on every hand.

Before I knew it my memory machine was functioning the way it's supposed to on a psychiatrist's couch, dredging up particulars, not just the rosy nostalgia that comes to mind when you hear an old song. Now don't get me wrong my memories are pretty happy and I enjoy closing my eyes now and then for a re-run or two. But I also find life exciting and good today, in truth better in most respects.

I looked at these young people and wanted them to feel

good about the world they've inherited. They'd already covered such things as present day pollution, our grasping materialism and the commercial rip-off in modern day merchandising. So for a little while they heard about the old nightly chore of banking the coal furnace (shoveling ashes on the fire to keep the coals alive through the night). The cold early morning journey to the basement to shake the grate, uncover the embers and shovel in coal and dressing in the shivering cold while you waited for the house to warm. As for their worry about air pollution—they were reminded that in that earlier time every chimney in town belched black smoke and soot every day from fall 'til summer.

Having been born in a small country town I could also tell them of that nighttime walk through the snow to that little wooden building out back of the house—a journey repeated in the morning. Summer brought the flies incubated in those outhouses of which there was one for every home and store and public building.

I went on about the apple barrel in the cellar, the ice box, the lack of fresh vegetables in winter etc. But let me go back a century or more so this won't just be a personalized trip down memory lane.

Dr. John J. McKetta, Chairman of the National Air Quality Commission, has written an essay which does much to set the record straight on pollution and related subjects. In passing he gives a capsule description of the really good old days about 150 years ago.

"For one thing," he says, "life was short. Life expectancy

for males was 38 years." It was a hard 38 years too for the work week was 72 hours. For women it was even worse, their household chores ran to about a 98 hour week. They scrubbed floors by hand, made clothes the same way, brought in firewood, cooked in heavy iron pots and fought off insects without pesticides.

There were no fresh vegetables except in their season of ripening so vitamin deficiency diseases were common. Epidemics were an annual occurrence and usually claimed the life of someone in the family. If we think water pollution is a problem now—it was deadly then. One typhoid epidemic in Philadelphia caused by polluted water carried off one-fifth of the population.

It was a time when most people never traveled more than 20 miles from their birthplace, never heard an orchestra, or saw a play. As Dr. McKetta says, "Perhaps the simple life was not so simple."

Because we've all been treated to so much misinformation about pollution I'm going to give you some more of the facts the doctor has collected in the next couple of days. I think you'll be surprised and relieved because he says and proves that we are not on the brink of ecological disaster.

Freedom
November 8, 1977

Sometimes I wonder if we haven't talked freedom, free enterprise etc. so much and so long as abstract theory that people—particularly young people—don't just tune us out. Speaking to some students the other day I referred to freedoms lost in this land during my lifetime. And I got a question—what freedoms? What was I talking about?

It reminded me of a TV play I'd once done in which I played a Soviet major during the occupation of Budapest. In the play I turned out to be something of a nice fellow and let two Hungarians go with this line, "I never knew what freedom was until I saw you lose yours."

But facing these students I had to search for an answer. This is what I came up with: when I was their age there was no such thing as a driver's license. Your father began teaching you to drive the family car when he thought you were old enough and after you'd driven him crazy asking why weren't you old enough.

You passed your driver's test when he said, "Yes you can take the car on your date tonight." Believe me he didn't say that until he was as sure as it's possible to be that you knew how to drive.

Now maybe you'll say that's not a good example; that driver's licenses are a necessity. Are there any fewer accidents today than there were then? Is there a better test of your ability than a parent turning you loose at the wheel of several thousand dollars of investment of hard earned money? What about twelve-year-old farm kids driving tractors on their father's farm and plowing a field yet?

Well this led to other examples. When I was fourteen years old I got a summer job with an outfit that was rebuild-

Radio Freedom

The other day I told a group of students that my wish for them was that they could know in this land the freedom I had known when I was their age.

I'll be right back.

Some times I wonder if we haven't talked freedom, free enterprise etc. so much & so long as abstract theory that people — particularly young people dont just tune us out. Speaking to some students the other day I referred to freedoms lost in this land during my life time. And I got a question — what freedoms? what was I talking about?

It reminded me of a T V play I'd once done in which I played a Soviet Major during the occupation of Budapest. In the play I turned out to be some thing of a nice fellow and let two Hungarians go with this line; "I never knew what freedom was until I saw you lose yours."

But facing these students I had to search for an answer. This is what I came up with; when I was their age there was no such thing as a drivers license. Your father began teaching you to drive the family car when he thought you were old enough and after you'd driven him crazy asking why weren't you old enough.

You passed your drivers test when he said "Yes you can take the car on your date tonite". Believe me he didn't say that until he was as sure as it's possible to be that you knew how to drive.

Now maybe you'll say that's not a good example; that drivers licenses are a necessity. Are there any fewer accidents today than there were then? Is there a better test of your ability than a parent turning you loose at the wheel of several

thousand dollars investment of his hard earned
money? What about 12 yr. old farm kids driving
tractors on their fathers farm & plowing a field yet?

Well this led to other examples. When I was
14 yrs. old I got a summer job with an outfit
that was rebuilding & selling old homes. Before the
summer was over I had laid hard-wood floor,
shingled roof, painted & worked on foundations.
And at summers end I had my first years tuition
for college in the bank. Can that be done today?
No! You'd have to get a govt. license first about every
kind of work I did. And just as it does with driving,
govt. not the person who hires you would decide whether you were capable.

In a recent debate with Ralph Nader a
distinguished scholar recently threw the obvious
example of lack of freedom at Ralph & did so
deliberately, sure of the answer he'd get. "What
right" he challenged "does govt. have to say you
cant ride a motorcycle without a helmet? You
aren't endangering anyone but yourself?"

Right on came a typical Naderism. If a helmet
less rider splashes himself on the pavement, a
govt. subsidized ambulance will pick him up, take
him to a govt. subsidized hospital. If he dies he'll
be buried in a govt. subsidized cemetery and govt.
welfare will begin paying for the support of his
widow & orphaned children. Therefore govt cant let him
fall down & go boom. In other words we are
all now stamped — "Property of the U.S. Govt. Do
Not Fold, bend or mutilate".

This is RR. Thank you for listening.

ing and selling old homes. Before the summer was over I had laid hardwood floor, shingled roof, painted and worked on foundations. And at summer's end I had my first year's tuition for college in the bank. Can that be done today? No! You'd have to get a government license to do just about every kind of work I did. And just as it does with driving, government not the fellow who hired you would decide whether you were capable.

In a recent debate with Ralph Nader a distinguished scholar recently threw the obvious example of lack of freedom at Ralph and did so deliberately, sure of the answer he'd get. "What right," he challenged, "does government have to say you can't ride a motorcycle without a helmet? You aren't endangering anyone but yourself?"

Right on cue came a typical Naderism. If a helmet-less rider splashes himself on the pavement, a government subsidized ambulance will pick him up, take him to a government subsidized hospital. If he dies he'll be buried in a government subsidized cemetery and government welfare will begin paying for the support of his widow and orphaned children. Therefore government can't let him fall down and go boom. In other words we are all now stamped—"Property of the United States Government. Do Not Fold, Bend or Mutilate."

Reagan's Own Life in Stories and Humor

REAGAN ENJOYED TELLING STORIES ABOUT HIS EARLY YEARS. THE FIRST THREE SELECTIONS WERE WRITTEN IN THE WHITE HOUSE IN RESPONSE TO REQUESTS. THE LAST SELECTION, ABOUT HIS EXPERIENCES IN HOLLYWOOD, WAS WRITTEN WHEN HE WAS ONLY 26.

In this letter Reagan responds to a request for more information about his early life.

Reagan's Huck Finn Years
May 22, 1984

Dear John:

I'm afraid all I can come up with in the line of photos of the "younger" days is this shot of me as a lifeguard in Dixon.

A younger, bow-tied Reagan, long before he entered the political arena.

I'm returning the two you sent in case you need them. Everything we have is in storage with all our furniture in California and to tell you the truth I can't recall if there are any albums etc. We lost a number of things like that in the Bel Air fire.

If you meant other pictures—Hollywood, Sacramento, the ranch or here let me know. Those I can deliver.

You asked for more information; well we left Tampico while I was still a baby—around two years old. We lived in Chicago then Galesburg and Monmouth (both in Illinois). I started school in Galesburg, only went to first grade there. Then we returned to Tampico and lived above Pitney's store.

All this travel was because Jack's interest was in shoes and he kept moving for promotions in the shoe departments of department stores. In Chicago it was Marshall Fields. Our move to Dixon was because Pitney opened a shoe store and Jack became top man.

But those few years back in Tampico became my Huck Finn years. Across the street living above their store was the Winchell family. Their youngest son and I (same age) became buddies. We used to do a lot of hiking out to the Hennipen Canal or to a large sand pit which had been created by a tornado.

One Saturday night when the stores were open so our folks were working downstairs he and I were upstairs at Winchells. We found his father's shotgun. We put it butt down on the floor and he pulled the trigger. Nothing happened. Then I pumped it once and said now try it and he did. That produced the loudest bang we'd ever heard and a dishpan sized hole in the ceiling.

When two white faced parents fearful of what they might find, pushed open the door the two of us were sitting on the couch studying our Sunday School lesson to beat h—l — a perfect picture of innocence.

Well I'd better stop or I'll be doing my life story.

It's good to hear from you and I enjoyed your article on "When."

> Best Regards
> Ron

Reagan wrote this account while he was president in response to a request from UPI, which was doing a series of articles about famous Americans and their recollections of their first jobs.

Reagan's First Jobs
February 1984

If they mean the really first job it was a summer job at age fourteen. My brother and I had been told by our father that if we wanted to go to college we'd have to work our way. He'd do what he could to help but there was no way he could put up the entire cost.

Along about freshman year in high school I figured that meant getting summer jobs and saving money. A minister in our town had embarked on a side line, buying old houses and remodeling them for re-sale. He had a few skilled craftsmen—carpenters, plumber, electrician etc. I was none of these but I was hired at 35¢ an hour—ten hour day, six days a week. First tools handed me were pick and shovel.

The house being remodeled had no basement. While remodeling went on in the house above, three of us knocked a hole in the foundation and dug our way under the house and created a basement by hand. Every shovelful of dirt and rock had to be thrown out the hole in the foundation.

Before the summer was over I'd graduated to laying hardwood floor, shingling roof and painting the exterior. Believe me all of this stood me in good stead when we did most of the fixing up on our 100 year old ranch house ourselves.

I remember one incident very well in that first summer after we'd moved on to another remodeling job. I was back to pick and shovel—this time out in the open. I'd spent a long hot morning swinging that pick. I lifted it for another blow and at the top of my back swing the noon whistle blew. I never completed the chop. I just let go of the pick handle and stepped out from underneath as the pick fell behind me. And behind me I heard some unclergy-like language. Turning around—reluctantly—I saw our boss, the reverend standing there with the pick embedded in the ground between his feet.

Worst of all my father saw the whole incident having just driven up to give me a ride home for lunch. Yes in small towns working people go home for lunch.

Now if you mean what was my first job for real, after I graduated from college that's a different story.

I'd moved on from my construction work at age fifteen to lifeguarding at a river beach in a beautiful natural forest park owned by the city of Dixon. My employer was the concessionaire who operated beach, bathhouse and lunch stand.

Fresh out of college and broke I went back to one last summer of lifeguarding to get some job hunting money. This was 1932 and the very bottom of the great depression.

It probably seems strange in this day of school counselors and all but there I was with a degree in economics and sociology (known today as social science) and not the slightest idea of what I wanted to do career wise.

A rather successful executive in the corporate world, whose children I'd taught to swim gave me perhaps the best advice I've ever had. He told me if I could tell him what kind of business or work I'd like to get in he'd try to open some doors for me.

Now I had to look inside myself and see what it was I thought would be the kind of thing I'd like to do. I went back to him after several days of soul searching and told him I'd like to be a radio sports announcer.

Radio was the new industrial giant in America. Only a few years old it had made an impact on American life far greater than TV did in these more recent years. A whole new line or profession had come into being with the play by play description of every kind of sporting event. Names like Graham McNamee, Ted Huring, Quinn Ryan, Pat Flanagan and a half dozen more were nationally known.

The advice my friend gave me was prefaced with the line

that he had absolutely no connections with anyone in radio and therefore could open no doors there. But then he added, maybe that was better; that anyone he might have sent me to would be doing him a favor more than having an interest in my future.

His advice was that I should simply start knocking on radio station doors asking for any job simply to get into radio; that my ambition was sports announcing but I believed in the future of radio and wanted to be a part of it and would take any job just to get on the inside. He reminded me that salesmen sometimes have to make 200 calls before they make a sale so I shouldn't get discouraged. He said somewhere I'd meet an employer who knew even in those terrible depression days that he had to prepare for the future by having young people coming along.

I took his advice. I hitchhiked to Chicago and knocked on every door. Chicago was a great center of radio in those early days. In one stop a kind lady in the program department encouraged me to keep looking but said I should get out of the city and try some of the smaller cities where they could better afford to take on someone without experience.

I left Chicago, knocked on doors across Illinois and crossed the river into Iowa. At WOC Davenport I made my standard pitch and this time the turn down was accompanied by word that I was a week late. They had held auditions and hired an announcer the week before.

That was too much. On the way out I said aloud, "how do you get to be a sports announcer if you can't get inside a radio station." The door closed behind me and I went down the hall to the elevator. While I was waiting for it I heard someone calling. It was Peter MacArthur the program director I'd been talking to. He was severely crippled by arthritis and was making his way down the hall with the help of two canes.

When he caught up with me he asked what was that I'd just said about sports announcing. I repeated what I'd said and he asked me if I knew anything about football. When I told him I'd played it for eight years he asked if I thought I could tell him about a game and make him see it. I said I thought so. With that he took me into a studio, stood me in front of a mike and told me to broadcast an imaginary game, that he would be in another room listening to it. I was to start when the red light went on and with that I was alone.

I knew I had to have names so I decided I'd do the fourth quarter of a game I'd played in my last year at Eureka which we won on a 65 yard touchdown run in the last 20 seconds. I knew all the names on our own team and remembered enough of the other teams to get by. And with that the red light went on. Fifteen minutes later I called the final gun and then grabbed the mike to keep from falling down. My knees had suddenly gotten very wobbly.

Peter MacArthur came back in the studio and said; "Be here Saturday you are broadcasting the Iowa-Minnesota game. You'll get $5 and bus fare." I was a sports announcer. I finished the Iowa season at $10 a game and bus fare and then was taken on as a staff announcer.

One of the best kept secrets about Reagan is how much he wrote even while President, including his two inaugural addresses and a number of major policy speeches. Here he is at work in his White House study.

Everything my friend had told me worked out the way he said it would.

While he was president, Reagan chatted with Owen Ullmann, the reporter covering the White House for Knight-Ridder, about jokes and joke-telling at a get-together for reporters. Ullmann requested the President's three favorite jokes for an article he planned to write on Reagan's story-telling expertise.

Reagan used many one-liners in broadcast speeches, but he saved his favorite jokes for smaller, live audiences so that he could tell them again on other occasions. It is rare to find his favorite jokes in his own words, let alone his own hand.

Three Favorite Jokes
August 5, 1986

I assume he [Ullmann] means stories suitable for use in speeches—there are many stories that are humorous but not suitable for that kind of situation.

1. This has to do with explaining the importance of brevity in a speech. A young, newly ordained minister was invited to preach at an evening service in a country church out in Oklahoma. It was his first sermon. He worked on it for days. Then came the night and he stood up in the pulpit and faced a church empty except for one lone fellow among all the empty pews. After the opening music the young preacher went down and said to the man: "Look

I'm just a young preacher getting started and you seem to be the only member of the congregation that showed up: What do you think? Should I go through with it?" The fellow said: "Well I don't know much about that sort of thing. I'm just a little old cowpoke out here in Oklahoma. But I do know this; if I took a truck load of hay out on the prairie and only one cow showed up—I'd feed her."

Well the preacher took that as a cue and delivered his sermon. An hour and a half later he said, "Amen." He went down and said, "Well my friend you seem to have stuck with me—what do you think?" The cowpoke said, "Well like I told you I'm just a little cowpoke out here in Oklahoma and I don't know much about that sort of thing: But if I took a load of hay out on the prairie and only one cow showed up—I sure as h—l wouldn't give her the whole load."

2. A young fellow of Irish heritage was in court suing for $4 million. He was bandaged from head to toe and said he couldn't move a muscle as a result of an accident. He won the suit. The lawyers for the insurance company went over to him and said: "You're never going to enjoy a penny of that money. We know you're faking and we're going to follow you 24 hours a day. The first time you make a move we'll have you." The lad said: "Will you now? Well let me tell you what's going to happen to me. They're taking me out of here on a stretcher. Downstairs they're putting me in an ambulance which is tak-

ing me straight to Kennedy airport. There they're putting me on a plane that's taking me to Paris, France. In Paris they're putting me in another ambulance which is taking me to the Shrine of Lourdes. And there you're seeing the greatest miracle you ever saw."

3. A fellow driving down the highway at about 50 miles an hour suddenly noticed a chicken running along beside him. He stepped his speed up 'til he was doing about 70 and the chicken was still right beside him. Then the chicken sprinted ahead, passed him and turned into a lane. He made a sharp turn and went down the lane. He ended up in a barnyard. An old farmer was standing there. The driver asked him if he'd seen a chicken go by. The old boy said, "Yep it's one of mine." The driver said, "Tell me, am I crazy or did that chicken have three legs?" The farmer said: "Yep—I breed 'em that way." Well the driver asked him why and the fella said; "Well me and Ma both like the drumstick and when Junior came along, he liked the drumstick too. We got tired of fighting over them so I started raising them with three legs." The driver asked:—"How do they taste?" The farmer said: "Don't rightly know. We haven't been able to catch one."

Reagan left Des Moines, Iowa, for Hollywood in 1937 with a movie contract in his pocket. Before leaving he arranged to write a series of 17 articles for the Des Moines Sunday Register *about becoming a movie actor. They were published weekly beginning June 13, 1937. Here are a few short takes from the articles.*

Hollywood
June–October, 1937

We knocked off for lunch at 12:35 [it was Reagan's first day of filming] and I met and ate with Wayne Morris, Walter Catlett, Hugh Herbert and Frank Craven. . . . Herbert's even funnier off the screen than on, and that's saying something. . . . He's a grand fellow and gave me a lot of advice about doing things my own way instead of listening to every Tom, Dick and Harry I meet.

"A lot of people will tell you what to do," he said. "But if you're going to stand out, you've got to do things the way it comes naturally to you. Otherwise you'll be just a robot, without any personality and those actors are a dime a dozen out here."

It's good advice, and I'm going to remember it.

That evening, after dinner at the Wards' [George Ward was Reagan's agent], we went to the midget auto races at Gilmore stadium. It seems to be one of the places on everybody's calendar as I saw dozens of screen stars there. The races were very thrilling and those little bugs sure can travel.

I got a real pang of homesickness at those races. I looked

A rising movie star in the late 1930s, Reagan was seductively handsome, the idol of thousands of young movie fans who wrote to him requesting a photo—and he obliged.

up at the press box where the boys were laughing and kidding each other and for the first time I realized I was only a guy in the grandstand now and not a member of the working press. Believe me, it was quite a wrench.

—June 20, 1937

I was instructed to go to the make-up department for a final going over to get my makeup set for the duration of *Inside Story* . . . Clay Campbell, make-up man, started in on my face then and in walked Olivia de Havilland, utterly ignoring me as she removed her eye-lashes and chatted with Campbell. I simply sat there with my mouth open, and she walked out.

Campbell discussed what to do with my haircut, and after a couple of trials decided that whereas I'd always parted my hair in the middle, from now on it should be parted on the side.

I told him I'd been wanting to meet some of the stars, especially Olivia who is my idea of really something, and before I could stop him he'd stepped to the door and shouted, "Liver!"

"Hello," a sweet voice answered when Campbell asked her to step in for a minute, the beautiful Olivia, all unsuspecting, came in, her hair wrapped in a towel and her face smeared with cold cream. A kimono was flung tightly around her shoulders.

"Olivia, a new Warner Bros. player wants to meet you. This is Miss de Havilland, Mr. Reagan," the make-up man introduced. Olivia was so confused she sputtered: "Oh dear, such a way to meet a stranger," and grabbing her kimono around her, fled from the room.

I was sort of embarrassed myself, being about half made up and with my shirt off, but Campbell just laughed like he thought it was a good joke.

—June 27, 1937

The night ended [Reagan has filmed a night scene] at sun-up and at 5 a.m., I drove back home through the winding California hills, experiencing the thrill of my first sunrise in many months. And boy, when it comes up over the rise of mountains that hedge in Hollywood on the east, with the misty clouds radiating all the colors of the rainbow, it's something to write home about. Which I guess is just what I'm doing.

—July 18, 1937

There's nothing like a good word from home to cheer a fellow up when he's beginning to wonder if it's worthwhile to give up all his friends and start fresh in a field entirely different from anything he has ever known.

So you may imagine how elated and happy I am to have a whole bundle of mail from friends and well wishers, especially from Iowa. They came along just at a time I was feeling a bit low, having finished my first picture, *Love Is on the Air,* for Warner Bros. and was trying vainly to peer into the future and see what it held in store.

—August 1, 1937

[Reagan has the part of Sergeant Riley in a movie, *Sergeant Murphy*, about a talking horse.]

Following instructions, I dived head first under the hoofs of the excited, prancing horse, rolling in ankle deep dust and dirt. . . . I'd much rather not have made that dive. I'm no hero, but it was the director's idea of the proper action and I had to do it or else.

In the few months I've been working for Warner Bros. I've become hardened to this sort of business. You've got to do it if you're going to stick with pictures. If you're yellow and refuse to risk a few bruises or occasionally take a chance on something more serious you might as well pack your bags and leave Hollywood.

It's a tough racket but when you consider the rewards you're shooting at—fame such as couldn't be won in any other profession and wealth that mounts to dizzying heights—it's worth the chances you take.

—August 22, 1937

I've been the victim of a dirty trick—making a personal appearance at a preview of my first picture—and if I never go through another experience like that for a hundred years it will be too soon.

Without warning I was asked by Eddie Selzer, the Warner Brothers publicity director, if I wanted to do him a favor. Being that kind of a guy, I said, "Sure," and never went into the details. He explained the manager of a theater in Huntington Park had staged a neighborhood beauty contest and wanted me to present the cup to the winner.

It wasn't until the main title was suddenly flashed on the screen that I realized I had been hornswoggled into not only seeing myself in *Love Is on the Air,* but also that I had agreed to step up in front of that audience after it had seen my first efforts as an actor and take a chance that they'd throw anything that was loose in my direction.

When the title, *Love Is on the Air,* followed with the list of the cast, came on the screen, I almost died. If I had had some warning, it might have helped.

I tried to appear nonchalant, but I am sure I only looked sick. The theater was dark so no one knew. It didn't help my hollow-leg feeling either, when a publicity man sitting beside me whispered, "This is the toughest preview spot in the world. I've seen them boo pictures here and walk out in droves."

My suffering increased as the picture unwound and I kept sliding down in my seat until I could scarcely see over the people in front of me. They tell me that all the tortures I went through are typical reactions everyone has when he sees his first picture in public. "A guy has to have a lot of nerve after going through that to go out and make another one."

I was agreeably surprised, at the finish, to hear the audience burst into applause but I was still mopping my brow a few minutes later when the beauty contestants were lined up on the stage and I was called up to the microphone. Luckily I had spotted Eddie Acuff, my partner in the picture, seated in the audience and I dragged him along with me. With him as moral support we clowned through the contest and got away without having anything thrown at us.

I grabbed the trade papers the first thing next morning to read the worst about myself and prepared to pack my trunk for the return trip back home.

But whether they were kidding me or not, they had nothing but words of praise. One paper went so far to say, "Warner Bros. have a new find in Ronald Reagan, young leading man, who promises to go places."

I'd been promising myself to forget acting and go home, but decided they didn't mean that so I guess I'll stick around and see what happens. If the studio and the fans can stand it, I certainly can, too.

—September 19, 1937

With *Accidents Will Happen* finished, I'm in the market for a house and already have a list of 15 real estate agents.

I'm bringing my parents, Mr. and Mrs. John Edward Reagan, out from the old family home in Dixon, Ill., now that it looks like I've got a permanent job—for at least six months more—and for the first time in several years I'm going to get my feet under the table and enjoy food "just like mother used to make."

And am I happy!

—October 3, 1937

Reagan's Own Life in Stories and Humor • 119

Acknowledgments

THE IDEA FOR THIS BOOK came from Bruce Nichols, our editor at The Free Press. In our first book, *Reagan, In His Own Hand,* we focused on Ronald Reagan's writings on foreign and domestic policy. Bruce noticed that some of Reagan's unpublished writings were personal and philosophical rather than policy oriented, and suggested we consider a small book focusing on them.

As we moved further into examining and publishing the large cache of private papers written by Reagan, we were greatly helped by a substantial grant from Tad Taube, a member of the Hoover Institution's Board of Overseers, and another generous grant from William Lane, the former ambassador to Australia under President Reagan.

Throughout the project, as was true for our first book on these papers, we had the full support and cooperation of

Nancy Reagan, who feels even more strongly today that the handwritten documents of Ronald Reagan are essential to an accurate and full understanding of the man and his legacy.

George Shultz has been our advisor and sounding board throughout, writing the telling foreword and providing the sketches that Reagan drew during a high level foreign policy meeting in Bonn, Germany, in 1984.

The Hoover Institution, led by John Raisian, has continued to support our work on the Reagan Papers project, including consultation and advice from Charles Palm, Richard Sousa, and Elena Danielson. Kiron Skinner also received generous support from the Department of History, the Department of Social and Decision Sciences, and the Office of the Dean of Humanities and Social Sciences at Carnegie Mellon University, and the John M. Olin Foundation.

Mark Burson, the executive director of the Ronald Reagan Presidential Foundation, and Joanne Drake, chief of staff to President Reagan, provided valuable assistance in facilitating access to the papers and in negotiating the book contract. In addition, they were generous in sharing their knowledge of Ronald Reagan and counseling us on numerous matters.

The professional staff of the Ronald Reagan Presidential Library continued to be helpful at all stages of the project, especially R. Duke Blackwood, the director; the archivists— Diane Barrie, Kelly Barton, Steve Branch, Greg Cumming, Mike Duggan, Sherrie Fletcher, Shelly Jacobs, Lisa Jones,

Cate Sewell, and Jenny Sternaman; and the technicians David Bridge and Josh Tenenbaum.

Anne Hawkins, our agent, provided crucial advice and counsel at every step of the project.

Karen Walag did most of the work of carefully transforming Reagan's handwritten drafts into the final typed manuscript. Brenda McLean also typed some of the manuscript. Susan Schendel proofread the final manuscript. Jong Lee and Molly Molloy checked and confirmed the accuracy of many of the stories.

Others who gave us advice, read parts of the manuscript, and made suggestions include Byron Skinner, Gloria Skinner, and Ruby Skinner.

The photographs of the handwritten documents shown in the book were taken by Brian Forrest.

The excerpt from Charles Edison's writings included in "Do Right" is published with the permission of the Charles Edison Fund.

Radio Charity

This I know will sound chauvinistic but the American people are the most generous people on earth. This has to be the result of our free way of life. It's in right hard.

Some 130 or 40 years ago a French philosopher came to America to see at first hand what he called this great experiment. He's probably been quoted in these modern days more by after-dinner speakers than by others who share.

Going back to France he wrote a book about democracy in America. He said he had sought for the great secret of Am. in her ~~commerce~~ *commodius* harbors & her ample rivers & it was not there. Nor did he find it in our rich mines & vast world commerce. He wrote, " but until I went to the churches of Am. & heard her pulpits aflame with righteousness did I understand the secret of her genius & her power. Am. is great because she is good & if Am. ever ceases to be good, Am. will cease to be great."

In his book he told his countrymen how in Am. a citizen would see a problem that needed solving; that he wouldn't call on the govt; but would cross the street & talk to a neighbor. They would talk to others & soon a committee would be formed, the problem would be solved and as de Tocqueville said " you won't believe this but your govt. bureau will be involved at all."

Our French writer of more than a century ago would have been re-assured if he had been in Santa Barbara Calif. a short time ago. A young girl lovely in her teens faced certain death from a form of leukemia. Her chance for life depended on the relatively new & unusual procedure of bone marrow transplant. The operation and accompanying treatment available in a medical center in Minn. costs tens of thousands of dollars money which the family didn't have.

Word got around. Then the local media broke the story. Some one proposed forming a committee.